BOWIEODYSSEY75

Also by Simon Goddard

Bowie Odyssey 74
Bowie Odyssey 73
Bowie Odyssey 72
Bowie Odyssey 71
Bowie Odyssey 70
The Comeback
Rollaresque
Simply Thrilled
Ziggyology
Mozipedia
Songs That Saved Your Life

BOWIEODYSSEY75
SIMONGODDARD

OMNIBUS PRESS

London / New York / Paris / Sydney / Copenhagen / Berlin / Madrid / Tokyo

Note to the Reader: The following narrative takes place in 1975 and contains language and prevailing attitudes of the time which some readers may find offensive. The publishers wish to reassure that all such instances are there specifically for reasons of historical social context in order to accurately describe the period concerned.

Copyright © 2025 Omnibus Press
(A division of the Wise Music Group
14–15 Berners Street, London, W1T 3LJ)

Paperback cover image by Studiocanal Film/Alamy Stock Photo
Hardback cover image by Studiocanal Film/Alamy Stock Photo
Endpapers by Studiocanal Film/Alamy Stock Photo
Cover designed by Fabrice Couillerot
Art direction and picture research by Simon Goddard

Hardback ISBN 978-1-9158-4155-1
Paperback ISBN 978-1-9158-4156-8

Simon Goddard hereby asserts his right to be identified as the author of this work in accordance with Sections 77 to 78 of the Copyright, Designs and Patents Act 1988.

All rights reserved. No part of this book may be reproduced in any form or by any electronic or mechanical means, including information storage or retrieval systems, without permission in writing from the publisher, except by a reviewer who may quote brief passages.

Every effort has been made to trace the copyright holders of the photographs in this book but one or two were unreachable. We would be grateful if the photographers concerned would contact us.

A catalogue record for this book is available from the British Library.

Typeset by Evolution Design & Digital Ltd (Kent)
Printed in Poland.
www.omnibuspress.com

BOWIECONTENTS75

BOWIEODYSSEY75   1

DISCOGRAPHY   149
SOURCES   151
IMAGES   155
THANKS   157

'I suddenly started to see a lot of things very clearly and this coincided with the onset of what I suppose was a kind of nervous breakdown. I felt as if I was going sane and mad at the same time, but then the words sane and mad don't have much meaning.'

THE DEATH OF REGINALD PERRIN,
DAVID NOBBS, 1975

ONE

'HssshwssshDavidBowiesmum'

THEY MUMBLE IN WHISPERS thinking she won't be able to hear them. But for a woman of 61 she has remarkably sharp ears. And eyes. She spotted them the moment she picked up her basket in Sainsbury's. Two jittery shadows freezing to a standstill in her peripheral vision. She knew what was coming next. Trailing her at a fixed half-an-aisle's length, browsing nothing, talking behind cupped hands, conspicuous as inept plainclothes policemen. It's happened before and it will happen again, which is why she has learned to accept it.

Fame.

Not that she, Mrs Jones, is remotely famous. Slap her face on the front-page of a national tabloid and most people wouldn't have the faintest who she was. Most people outside this small corner of BR3, where years of squinting glances and nudging elbows in checkout queues, butcher's counters and behind hot breath misting the windows of school buses have made her a local star of Beckenham High Street.

'Her – *there!* – you'll never guess who that is.'

'Who?'

'David Bowie's mum!'

'*Nooo waaay!*'

The reaction is always the same. Shock. That the mother of David Bowie should look like somebody's mother and not the mother of a somebody. That she should appear so disarmingly of this planet, waltzing round the supermarket with her basket swinging off her elbow, picking up tins of Campbell's soup like any other middle-aged housewife. Shampoo-and-set, the lightest stroke of lipstick, chunky-buttoned coat, sensible shoes, fiddling with her purse at the till and counting her change to the exact halfpenny.

And yet out of this, out of her, from between those legs poking beneath that tweed skirt, popped the child who became David Bowie. A life that began somewhere under those woollens, in a once fertile womb where the collection of cells now worshipped all over the globe on record, stage and bedroom wall first began to multiply from one of her fertilised eggs. And were it not for that specific act of sexual intercourse in the baby-boom April of 1946 then there would be no 'Space Oddity', no 'Starman', no 'Jean Genie', no 'Rebel Rebel'. And if there wasn't, then the world and its young, male and female – thus denied the gospel according to Ziggy Stardust, with their hair uncoloured, ears unpierced, nails unpainted, eyebrows unshaved and genders unbending – would look so much sadder and uninviting. Because all of that, all of him, would never have existed were it not for *this* woman.

Her body, *her* desires, *her* orgasm, *her* ovaries.

The universe in its uncountable infinity of possibilities, the odds were one in a million billion trillion against. A microscopic fraction of a subatomic shift either way and it might have ended in non-conception, miscarriage, abortion, stillbirth, deformity or death. Instead, it ended in the beginning of the life of David Bowie.

Her flesh, *her* blood, *her* bones, *her* genes.

And so she has to contend with disbelieving strangers, following her down the street, over the Zebra crossing, around the supermarket. Just to see if they can see any of *him* in *her*.

The courageous ones even stop and ask.

'Sorry . . . but are *you* David Bowie's mum?'

Before she can answer, they already know. When she looks them in the eye. With *his* eyes. Quartz laser beams that once locked on their human target have much the same effect as Medusa. Then her lips part,

SIMON GODDARD

exposing her jagged teeth, as tightly crushed together as *his* teeth. And it's like looking at David Bowie blinking through someone else's face as if through the foam of a freshly splattered custard pie.

'Yes' is needless, though she says it anyway, with a smile always demure, always genuine. She cannot pretend she doesn't love it. The maternal pride, the flattery, but most of all the recognition. That the general public should love the fruit of her loins enough to give the widowed Mrs Margaret Mary Jones, informally 'Peggy', all this attention.

Until they ask what they always ask.

'How is he?'

When the corners of her mouth twitch and her eyes flicker like a faulty lightbulb. When that demure yet genuine smile becomes the straining grimace of a politician.

'David's very busy. He's in America just now.'

Then braces herself for the inevitable.

'When's he coming back?'

When her lips wobble.

'Soon, I hope,' she says. 'This year. Soon.'

And her teeth clench as she can only repeat.

'Soon, I hope.'

Today's amateur sleuths aren't nearly so bold, content playing peekaboo behind soap powder packets, spying on her all the way to the till until she collects her receipt, thanks the cashier and turns left out of the door, up the high street and out of their starstruck sight. When the enigma of 'David Bowie's mum' vanishes into the grey pedestrian underworld and becomes plain old Mrs Jones again. But that's fame. A trick of the light blinding only the eye of the beholder.

Anonymous and unaccosted, Peggy carries her shopping up Albemarle Road, passing skeletal winter trees standing sentry to her loneliness, into her block of flats, up the stairs to the first floor, jingling her keys, slipping inside and locking the door behind her. No one to welcome her home except the phantom perfume of her morning cigarettes and the eyes of the famous son she hasn't seen in nearly a year, hanging on the wall, in tabletop picture frames, on record sleeves stacked over in the corner. Her private torture chamber of filial abandonment.

Beside her armchair, the plastic telephone she last spoke to him on, not quite two weeks ago. It was the first time he'd rung in almost nine months and it made her Christmas.

David was sniffing a lot. She asked if he'd caught a cold. He said he was fine, but he sounded tired, and she told him so.

He explained he'd been very busy recording. She told him he was working too hard.

He said it was all in hand and not to worry because he was parting company with Mr Defries. She said she was relieved to hear it since she'd always thought Defries 'an awful man'. David made a strange noise that might have been a laugh.

She asked after her grandson, there spending Christmas with him. He said Zowie was enjoying playing with his dad's video equipment and that Angie, his wife, would soon be back in London for New Year.

Peggy thought he'd want to know about her eldest, his half-brother, Terry. She'd just been to visit him in the local psychiatric hospital, Cane Hill. He was quite happy but forever asking after David. Would it hurt him to write to Terry once in a while?

The line went quiet.

'David?' she said.

'Yes,' he sniffed.

Changing the subject, he asked if she'd liked his Christmas present. She told him she was thrilled to bits with it.

Then, out of the blue, he said it.

'I love you, Mum.'

And Peggy cried.

His Christmas present. It's hanging in her wardrobe. Factory fresh and still unworn beyond a few twirls in the bedroom mirror. A mink coat. Thousands of pounds' worth of skinned mammals and she thinks it's smashing. Only a 61-year-old pensioner living on eleven quid fifty a week can't exactly totter down to Sainsbury's in three grand's worth of fur coat. Not unless she wants to be called 'Lady Muck' and jeered at all the way home. And so it remains on its hanger beside her inexpensive dresses and woollen cardies, a luxurious obscenity mocking her with its impractical uselessness. There, every day, to remind her of the poverty of wealth as a substitute for affection.

She thought he might ring her again yesterday, on his birthday. He was 28 and she sent a card by airmail care of his hotel in New York. But she sat in all night watching *This Is Your Life* with conductor Geoff Love and his surprise guest Max Bygraves, and the receiver never twitched.

It's the same most nights. Home alone in front of the TV, a glass ashtray perched on her armrest, an Embassy never far away from her lips, the phone deafeningly silent. If she wants to hear his voice, her only solace lies in his records, piled beside the stereo. Only every time she does, she just sits there, in pieces. Howling.

Through her window, the dusk light is rapidly fading. The early January nights are abyss black by half past four. The darkness still dark. The world still descending hellwards, like it says on the radio. *Down, down, deeper and down.*

Tonight, Peggy could watch the news with Kenneth Kendall, but it'd be too depressing, or *The Two Ronnies*, but she wouldn't laugh, or that new police drama the papers are raving about, *The Sweeney*, but it'd be too coarse for her. So the telly is switched off and the record player switched on. She picks the album at the front of the pile with her then-shaggy-haired son surrounded by blue dots on the front. She fumbles with the gatefold, slides the vinyl out of its inner sleeve, places it on the turntable then presses the cue button. The stylus rises and glides into position as she walks back to her armchair. By the time her buttocks have sunk in her cushion she can hear the crackles. Then, faint at first, growing gradually louder, the dismal swipes of a minor key acoustic guitar.

'*Ground control . . .*'

And her floodgates burst.

But in her torrents roll many rivers of secret pain.

On the surface, the fast-flowing shallows of a mother bereft, sentimentally boohooing over the sweet little boy that was and the aching distance that is: a distance more than physical, measurable only in strange longitudes of emotionless unfeeling stretching to infinity.

Yet beneath, where the current slows, where the light is weak and the water cloudy, the jealous depths of a life denied. The grief for what might have been had young Peggy Burns herself followed her girlish daydreams of becoming a singer – a *somebody* – instead of a mother. A mother David would never love as much as his now-dead father, even if *she* was the one who bequeathed him the art. Her dad, the army bandmaster, who played the clarinet. Her mum, who kept a notebook in her apron full of private poems testifying her melancholy. Words and music, melody and self-expression, trickling down the generations from them, through her, to him. Trickling like the rivulets cascading down her cheeks, if she even knows what it is she's crying for.

The son she's lost to fame?

Or the fame she lost because of her son?

A fame that now torments her with its cold leftover table scraps, in strangers stalking her around supermarkets and parcels from fans who've somehow found her address so they can send their wonky paintings of Ziggy, naively believing he'll see them himself on his next visit to his dear old ma.

From the darkened street, hers is a dim orange light behind drawn curtains, hanging in the moonless night like a little capsule adrift in its own helpless orbit. Just like the one David is singing about through her speakers, the sound of his voice chafing at her heart like a hacksaw as she sobs and bubbles swathed in stylophone moans and a fog of cigarettes.

A mother, lost in space.

HER SON, LOST IN SPACE.

David sees clusters of stars and twinkling nebulas, spiral galaxies, planets ringed by rainbows, fleets of luminous jellyfish-like flying saucers and faraway suns piercing the infinite indigo-black nothingness between with their thousand-year-old light. Sees it through the giant oblong windows of a spacecraft piloted by elflike star maidens with braided blonde hair, stripey purple leggings and calf boots with golden soles, swivelling on egg chairs as they gently monitor their bejewelled Technicolor dashboard. Sees it with eyes fizzing like a glass of Alka-Seltzer from all the white comets streaking through his veins. Sees the cosmos stretching out before him and knows he is standing at the heart of it. Sees it all and knows he definitely isn't dreaming.

All of this is real. Real as the music buzzing in his ears.

'Across the universe . . .'

Real as the mural on the studio walls.

Poor Jimi. This was supposed to be *his* spaceship. The one painted by artist Lance Jost to transform a former basement club in Greenwich Village into Jimi's personal pangalactic recording oasis. Electric Lady. Only by the time Lance swiped his first brushstroke Jimi was sleeping the big sleep in the same Seattle graveyard as his mother. He never got to see it. Never got to feel what David feels, standing here, below the New York sidewalk, travelling interstellar. Kissing the sky.

On West 8th Street, he isn't alone. Up the stairs, outside and next door to the studio is the Playhouse cinema. This week's feature, 'all seats $1', an oldie but goodie. Seven years old and still pulling in the potheads.

Seven years ago, David was one of them. Twenty-one and not yet famous, anonymous and unaccosted as he danced on cannabis through still-swinging London streets of felt hats and Afghan coats, up Leicester Square between *Doctor Zhivago* at the Empire and the Chicken Inn, into Soho's non-stop beat of strippers and chop suey, right along Old Compton, serenaded by the ching-chings of sixpences gobbled by the bandits of the Golden Goose, swerving a black cab as he crossed Frith to the gleaming box office of the Cinerama Theatre. Where *2001: A Space Odyssey* peeled his eyeballs like oranges.

That's how it all started for David in the summer of '68. Without the cosmic whiplash of Kubrick's Super Panavision he'd have never written 'Space Oddity', the song that launched him, that set him on his fated trajectory so that one day, many years later, he'd find himself in New York City, in a studio built for Jimi Hendrix, staring at painted galaxies sat next to his new pal, John, while *2001* plays next door like a crossed stitch in time to remind David how he got here. Through the Star-Gate. Beyond the Infinite. Across the Universe.

His new pal, John. Formally, Dr 'Winston O'Boogie' Lennon. Here on the sofa, tapping a foot, face curtained by long hair wedged under a floppy newsboy cap, light bouncing off the granny glasses perched atop his shinbone of a nose making him look like a startled macaque. He has a light Florida tan from Disney World where he spent Christmas riding the monorail and signing the legal documents to finally dissolve The Beatles. No one has to remind John how *he* got here.

Not even the United States Immigration and Naturalization Service, though every so often they enjoy reminding him he has to leave.

BOWIEODYSSEY75

The cancer of his liberty, the never-ending fight for his Green Card. Until it's sorted John can never go home to England as they'd never let him back in again. So he stays, and appeals, and quietly pines for black pudding and Chocolate Olivers, getting drunk, getting sober, getting high, coming down, watching TV, movies and the odd flying saucer, laying low, entertaining the few friends he has and making music any chance he gets. Like this one.

He's only known David a few months. Not that he *knows* him. Not that he's sure David even does himself. The Andes John's seen him chopping out it's not surprising. Whole South American valleys vanishing up his nostrils, one hillside at a time. No wonder he looks like a locust. And how can anyone really be on intimate terms with a locust?

Still, here he is because David asked him, because while John shuns the spotlight he still loves the studio, and because it's his song.

'Across The Universe'.

Of all the songs he's ever written he can't think why David should want to sing that one when he never made a proper job of it himself. And maybe eighteen months ago he'd have said no. But times, and John, have changed. Last year Elton begged him to join him on a cover of 'Lucy In The Sky With Diamonds'. John obliged, and it's America's number 1 this week, the second he's had in a year. The other was his own 'Whatever Gets You Thru The Night', where Elton returned the favour, playing piano and betting John that if it got to the top he'd have to join Elton on stage. It did and he did, only a few weeks ago at Madison Square Garden. John was sick with nerves, but it only proved what the Justice Department somehow fail to understand. America *wants* Lennon.

So does David. Like a prize medal so he can run home from school and show off to the neighbours. Top of the form. Pride of our alley. Cock of the walk.

Look, Mum, I've made a record with a Beatle!

And not just *any* Beatle.

Johnny Beatle.

The Beatle.

You can hear it in his voice. That's not David singing 'Across The Universe'. It's hubris and the chemical landslide of dopamine that fed it. He chews every word till his gums bleed without understanding what any

8

of them mean, making a naval destroyer of a paper boat. And yet there sits John, calmly strumming his guitar, privately humming the Sanskrit lyrics David struck out, oblivious to the flaming ruins of his song of serenity falling around his head like a barn fire.

It's more than powdered narcissism. There's something else possessing David. A defiance, an anger, a fear. It's why he's making a war cry of John's peace offering. When David sings how nothing is going to change his world it's no longer the mantra of a trippy truthseeker bound for Rishikesh. It's a personal revolt against his bloodsucking oppressor. His monster. The one David's been carrying for five years, for four of them not realising his monster *was* a monster. If only he'd listened to his mother.

'That *awful* man!'

Tony Defries must be destroyed.

David's only problem is how to assassinate the master assassin. He's never been a killer before. At times a willing loader of bullets, but never a trigger-puller. That's been Defries's job, and why he hired him. And why the thought of doing to Defries what Defries has done to so many others knots his guts in a half Windsor. The dread of imminent battle. The same John has to live with 24/7, wondering whether his next day in court will be his last before they poke him on the first plane home with a one-way ticket in his trousers and a Border Security revolver in his back. The terror of losing versus the desperation to win. Like oil and water, shake them up as much as you like, it's the desperation that sinks while the terror floats thickly to the surface, coating David's every thought in its gloopy despair, spilling out of his mouth in black vomit diatribes of money, managers and the monsters both breed. So stupefied by the termites gnawing his septum, he even spills it out to John, forgetting he's preaching to the choir.

Dr Winston's got troubles enough even without his immigration status. His own monster, as sick symbiotic fate would have it the very man who taught Defries every dark art in the chiseller's bible. See, David, he's only wrestling contracts with the bastard son. Lil' Satan Jr. John's in a legal death grip with the actual Devil himself. Allen Klein.

The Beatles' former manager is suing John and fellow Fabs George and Ringo for the bank-robbing outrage of being made their former manager.

BOWIEODYSSEY75

Nobody does that to Klein, and as recompense he wants the monetary equivalent of their shrunken heads on spikes to play like a xylophone.

Bing! Bang! Bong!

Until he gets them, all John can do is wince as Klein's subpoenas stack up and spew his own vomit in song. It all splattered out on his latest album in 'Steel And Glass'. If a rock'n'roll star can't forget about it, they might as well sing about it.

That's not so easy for David. He never got to be where he is today – here in Jimi Hendrix's studio making records with John Lennon – by singing how it feels to be David Bowie. He got here by singing about starmen, genies and life on Mars. The closest he's come to singing from the heart is the soul album he made in Philadelphia last year, still in the can, where he finally scraped away the greasepaint and bawled aloud, *'Can I be real?'* The album he's already in the process of diluting and dismantling today in Electric Lady with his grotesque Beatles cover. And the dismantling isn't over.

His disassembly line has been pulled together from his last touring band. His two guitarists – Carlos, the bright and funky one, and Earl, the pinned and squealy one – and Roy Ayers' old rhythm section, Emir and Dennis.

Next door, kettle drums are booming and black cuboid monoliths drift noiselessly towards the gas giants of the outer solar system.

The night is young.

Under Jimi's moulded plaster ceiling, shaped like a descending UFO, Carlos dredges the one riff worth salvaging from an old R&B number David kicked around on his last tour, 'Foot Stompin''. A simple, repetitious dip flash that soon has the rest of the band pat-a-caking along like a chain gang, all pickaxes swinging four-on-the-floor, even John, vamping on his acoustic. Something about its wide-hipped rhythm reminds him of a favourite tune he keeps hearing on the radio: an infectious thumping shuffle cut in a studio just across the Hudson which he's been tempted to check out himself. As he strums along with Carlos, John can't help but sing it over the top, loud enough for the mic to pick up.

'Shame, shame, shaaame . . .'

When David short-circuits.

He doesn't her the *sh*. Just the *aaame*. Like the waspish buzz of an insect crawling inside his eardrum.

Aaaaame.

Focusing his thoughts like a telescopic lens until he sees it all, sharp as a diamond. The emptiness of the limo life. The insanity of stardom. The ripped-off mug's game of what it really means to be 'David Bowie' at the mercy of a monster like Defries. Staring him in the face all this time and it hadn't ever crossed his mind to sing about it. Not until a second ago when John showed him how. Well, didn't he just hear him?

'Faaame'.

TWO

THE CONNAUGHT CAN COUNT ITSELF LUCKY. Last night, terrorists committed drive-by machine-gun attacks on two central London hotels. It wasn't one of them. Unlike the bloodied foyers of the Carlton Towers in Knightsbridge and the Portman not half a mile away, today is just like any other Monday, its doormen starched stiff, its teak bannisters gleaming and its restaurant still boasting 'the best cooking in England', where a dark-haired woman bobs her way like a yacht through a sea of white cloth to a table of two, sits down and makes it three.

To the maître d' she is 'Miss Abbott', the talent agent. To her lunching companions, 'Maggie'. They, in turn, are her friends 'Si' – Mr Litvinoff, the executive producer of *A Clockwork Orange* – and 'Nic' – Mr Roeg, the director of *Performance* and *Don't Look Now*.

The menus are dealt, the specials recommended, the Foie de Veau Sauté Lyonnaise considered, the Filet de Sole Bonne Femme favoured, the Burgundy agreed, the cork popped, the wine tasted, the vintage approved, the measures generously poured and the small talk exhausted before the first sip. Then with an inquiring – 'Peter O'Toole?' – Mr Litvinoff raises his glass and commences business.

'Yes,' says Miss Abbott, clinking his. 'You said you'd a script for him?'

'We do,' says Mr Roeg and promptly thumps it upon the tablecloth before twisting it round so Miss Abbott can read the typed cover.

SIMONGODDARD

The Man Who Fell To Earth

'Ah,' says Miss Abbott.

'You know it?' asks Mr Roeg.

'The book, yes,' she nods. 'Read it a few years ago. Funnily enough, it was through Donald's brother. He'd optioned it and asked me to read it. Think maybe he wanted Jagger for the part, I can't quite remember.'

'So now *we've* got the option,' says Mr Litvinoff. 'It's a great book and it'll make a terrific movie. It's all in the casting.'

'You know the story, then?' starts Mr Roeg, cradling his hands. 'An alien comes to Earth from a dying planet that's paralysed by drought. It's a life-or-death mission to take water back to save his race. He can only do this by disguising himself as a human and raising millions of dollars by selling patents based on his advanced alien technology, the plan being if he makes enough he can invest in space travel and return home with water. Of course, it all goes drastically wrong. The longer he stays on Earth, the more corrupted by humanity he becomes. Eventually the authorities discover he's an alien and his mission is ruined. In the end he's a marooned lonely alcoholic, unable to ever go home again. It's science fiction, but the story's really very human, really very sad. An extraterrestrial tragedy.'

Mr Litvinoff straightens up as a waiter serves his fish gasping in a puddle of butter. 'The lead role is key,' he says, admiring the plate. 'Newton.'

'Thomas Newton,' clarifies Mr Roeg as his own liver and onions glide gracefully under his nose. 'They have to have something of the *other* about them. An alien in human skin. The audience must believe they've fallen to Earth from another planet.'

'Which is why we thought of O'Toole. It's all in the eyes.'

'Thing is, I do know Peter,' says Miss Abbott, slicing into her fillet. 'But I don't represent him. Though I'm afraid I can tell you for a fact he's not available. I only know as he's about to start a film with one of my clients in Mexico.'

Mr Roeg frowns. 'How long for?'

'He's there already, shooting another film. Once that one's finished, he starts the next with Charlotte. He's busy all through the summer.'

'So you don't think we can get O'Toole?'

BOWIEODYSSEY75

'I don't think you can, no. Who else had you in mind?'

Mr Litvinoff sighs, grasps the Puligny–Montrachet by the neck and one by one tops up their glasses.

'Well, Peter O'Toole . . .'

Glug, glug.

'. . . Peter O'Toole . . .'

Glug, glug.

'. . . or, failing that, Peter O'Toole.'

Glug, glug, glug.

Miss Abbott smiles, takes a sip then politely drops a bomb.

'What about Jagger?'

'*Mick* Jagger?' asks Mr Litvinoff.

'Yes. I still look after him.'

'Jagger?' repeats Mr Roeg, eyebrows flinching in surprise. 'Oh, no. He's not right at all.'

'He was super in *Performance*.'

'That was *Performance*. This is a whole different character. No, Mick's much too strong for it.'

'Strong?'

'Yes. Physically. Newton needs to be frail. Like his bones are made of glass. There's a scene where the girl picks him up and carries him into an elevator.'

At 'frail' Miss Abbott has it. She knows exactly who they need for *The Man Who Fell to Earth*. Someone also on her books, whose wife she's good friends with, who's always asking her to find a suitable film role for her husband. And this is a film so obviously *him* she as good as shouts his name across the table.

'DAVID BOWIE!'

Mr Roeg stares at her blankly, fork in mid-air, chewing slowly.

'He's another of mine,' she glows. 'He's skinny enough. He can do frail. He's acted before, he does mime and all sorts. He's a very, very theatrical performer. Oh, he'd be absolutely *perfect*.'

Mr Roeg finally swallows, clearing his throat, dabbing the corners of his mouth with his napkin. The next three words that pass his lips are neither what Miss Abbott nor anyone else involved in popular entertainment in the year 1975 might reasonably expect.

'Who's David Bowie?'

THREE

THE HOUSEWIVES OF CHELSEA AWAKE. Some earlier than others. Six thirty a.m., and as the night scrapes its dying heels through the muddy skies over Flood Street her eyes spring open like greyhound traps. They last closed at one thirty. Five hours' sleep is all she needs, sometimes even less. The few dreams she has between are the stuff of her downstairs bookshelves. No classics, no romance, just hardback upon hardback of military history. The battle of Trafalgar, the life of Field Marshal Earl Alexander, Albert Speer's inside account of the Third Reich. Her first conscious thought – War! And they're never won by the slumbering.

Her battle dress hangs fresh from the National Sunlight laundry in Fulham where she waited in line, the proud grocer's daughter for whom the great British queue is a sacrosanct institution. Today, £42 worth of beige linen, among a handful of garments recently plucked from the rails of her favourite outfitter, Mansfield Originals in Marylebone, all snapped up in a decisive 15-minute flurry. Victory, after all, belongs only to those who don't dither in the changing rooms.

Her flesh-coloured tights are Marks & Spencer, her black leather court shoes from K's along the King's Road, the silk scarf she knots around her neck from Jaeger at the top of her street.

Once armoured, she sits at her dressing table applying make-up as she would turn a salt mill. Two quick twists for flavour and done. Her face is otherwise bald and bloodless, like an unfinished portrait awaiting a sable brush to apply dimples of pulsing life and a pair of eyebrows.

Her hair – two weeks since last bleached, six since last permed, and only a few days till its next spruce at Chalmer's in Mayfair – she scrapes back from her scalp with the heavy brush from her Delina vanity set, like her hand mirror, framed in gold-tone metal embroidered with flying geese. A last squirt of Boots hairspray holds it in place like the plumed busby of a hussar, ready to battle the new day.

The new day doesn't stand a chance.

Half a grapefruit and a boiled egg flushed down with coffee is all she needs to break her fast before tying on her checked half-apron to cook her husband's, the director of an oil company who earns three times what she does as an MP. She will then handwash his dishes before seeing him off at the doorstep in the clothes she ironed after handing him his brolly and briefcase. Traditions are traditions and must not be tampered with. But even if feminism is a foreign word inside number 19, hers are the first arms to roll up their sleeves before painting the skirting boards and putting up shelves. Packing Denis off to work isn't an act of subservience, merely domestic dictatorship. Clothe him, feed him, shoo the bastard out from under her feet so she can untie her apron and return to the front.

The morning report in the *Mail* is as she hoped. The polls indicate she is *'ahead'* of her desperate deadbeat rival to become the new party leader. Another two weeks and two ballots and she'll have Ted's head on a plate, just sadly not on her beloved Chippendale salver, stolen last year among £5,000 of jewellery and silverware when her house was burgled while she was out campaigning in the spring general election. A bad start to a year that didn't get any better. Before she'd had time to fill in her insurance claim, her worsted gaberdine skirt was buffing the unfamiliar leather of the Opposition benches after she found herself on the losing side, now a mere 'Shadow' Secretary of State. Topping it all was her foot-shooting interview with *Pre-Retirement Choice* magazine, bragging how she, in her SW3 townhouse on her salary of £4,500, had been hoarding non-perishable goods in her pantry 'for years' as a means of saving the odd ten pence on tinned salmon to beat inflation. And overnight became the most hated woman in a bare supermarket-shelved kingdom united by sugar shortages and hunger.

But that was then, 1974.

This is 1975, and this is her year. Officially 'International Women's Year', not that her sex has anything to do with it. She will win not by virtue of it, but in spite of it. She says it herself.

'Forget that I'm a woman.'

And she's right. She isn't. Don't be fooled by the floral perfume and the string of pearls. Strain a little closer and you might just see the glistening fangs of the big bad wolf. For 1975 really *is* her year. The Year of the Monster.

'Gee, Grandma! What big teeth you have!'

Good morning, Maggie.

TWO STREETS AWAY, as Maggie puts out the empties for tomorrow's milkman, in Oakley Street there stirs another slightly groggier Chelsea housewife. House in that she lives in one, wife in that she's married, but that's as far as the rubber glove fits. She won't be cooking her husband breakfast since he's currently over 3,000 miles away, at this present hour in the act of climbing between the sheets with another woman. Just as she's woken up in the bed they once shared, which they never will again, with another man. But even if her husband *was* here, god forbid she should be slavishly scrambling his eggs in a pinafore at this hour.

'I AM VERY SERIOUS ABOUT RELATIONSHIPS, BUT I DON'T HAVE ANY NEED TO POSSESS ANYONE!'

No. She is an altogether different sort of hands–on go–getter, if no less dogged in her ambition than the one round the corner. The mistress of number 89 is not at war with anyone or anything. She comes in peace. It's just that hers is the kind of peace that plays at full volume.

'WHEN I WAS 14 SOMEBODY SAID I WAS VERY LOUD. I THOUGHT, "SHOULD I BE UPSET OR BE QUIET FROM NOW ON?" THEN I THOUGHT, "THEY CAN THINK I'M LOUD UNTIL THE COWS COME HOME, BECAUSE OTHERS THINK I'M NICE AND FUN!" SO I WASN'T GOING TO GET UPSET. I'D MUCH PREFER SOMEONE HAD A POSITIVE OR NEGATIVE REACTION TO ME THAN BE MEDIOCRE OR WISHY-WASHY!'

Today will put that philosophy to the acid test when she goes before the cameras of London Weekend Television. Before they roll, she will spend twice as much time on her face as Maggie spends at her nightly ironing board. Her own battle dress is no less considered: a veiled pillbox hat, tit-popping bodice dress and a pair of heels that on any other feet might easily induce vertigo. The field of combat – Russell Harty's Friday night LWT chat show where she's been invited as a guest despite having nothing to sell but herself and the name on a five-year-old wedding certificate.

'MARRIAGE IS THE DEATH OF FRIENDSHIP. IT'S THE WORST THING IN THE WORLD. PEOPLE TREAT YOU AS IF YOU ARE SOME STRANGE UNITY MADE IN HEAVEN – *ABSOLUTE BALONEY!*'

She may be blonde but she's anything but dumb. She knows she's only been asked on in lieu of, and to talk about, her infinitely more famous husband. It's all she's ever asked about. She can pick up the phone and land a centrespread in the tabloids any week she wants, and does, so long as she wears something sexy and talks about her husband. Neither require any effort on her part.

'I NEVER CONSIDERED MYSELF PRETTY BUT I ALWAYS KNEW I COULD GET MYSELF TOGETHER AND KNOCK PEOPLE'S EYES OUT!'

Only these days she doesn't do it *just* to flash her impressive calves and send *Express* readers into spluttering meltdowns answering the same fusty old questions about her open marriage.

'IF I ATTACHED ANY IMPORTANCE TO SEX, THEN I MIGHT CONSIDER BEING FAITHFUL, BUT I JUST DON'T THINK IT IMPORTANT. SEX IS VERY BORING AS A SUBJECT.'

The game is the same, but her rules have changed. With superstar hubby overseas and out of the picture it's just her now, and Fleet Street had better get used to it. She is a woman of endless imagination and infinite zeal. This is going to be *her* year, alright. 'International Women's Year', see? And her sex has absolutely *everything* to do with it.

She'll bring down the house in her own stage play about a young prostitute driven to suicide. Either that or drown in garlands for her lead role in a film about Ruth Ellis, the last woman to be hanged. Or, if

SIMONGODDARD

not, be hailed the greatest thing since Plath when she publishes her first collection of poetry.

Oh, she'll be *everywhere*! Billboards, front pages, magazine covers and chat shows – starting tonight. She's already made it happen for her husband. Why shouldn't it now happen for her? Even *he* says it must.

'IT WAS DAVID WHO SUGGESTED I SHOULD DO SOMETHING ON MY OWN.'

Good day, Angie.

NOT 300 YARDS FROM ANGIE'S HATBOX, down the far end of Oakley Street, stopping short before the Albert Bridge, you can hear the city stretch and yawn in the gathering hum of traffic along the Embankment. The winter sun is rising, letterboxes flap, toasters pop, satchels sling and radios boogie 'Never Can Say Goodbye'. London is awake and it feels like dancing.

Except here on Cheyne Walk. The curtains of number 19 do not twitch. A year ago they would have done, and the face at the window would have been 84-year-old Isabella. Nearly three decades widowed and alone, but her cats still to live for, a struggle as it was at her age lugging all those heavy tins of Whiskas jellymeat home from the shop. So come the day a nice young man offered to help her with her bags, she invited him in and made him a cup of tea. He sat and sipped and listened as she talked about the old days. It was nice to have some human company. 'Come back anytime,' she said.

And he did. Every few months, he'd knock and she'd give him fivers to go and buy more cat food. He'd return in no time with just what she'd ordered and all the right change. It was like having her own cat-feeding angel sent from heaven.

Until one Thursday, last February. Valentine's Day. When he knocked again.

Isabella, as she always did, opened her door on its chain. Seeing him through the gap, her first impulse was to smile. Only the muscles of her mouth couldn't quite make it. There was something about him. A rabid wildness in his eyes, as if she could somehow tell he'd just spent the past 72 hours in a Tooting mental hospital after a policeman found him drunk and psychotic, threatening to commit suicide. That's why she wouldn't let him in.

'I don't need anything today,' she stammered.

But her angel did, and after booting the door off its chain and strangling her in the hallway he got what he came for. He then dragged her semi-conscious body into the kitchen, took a 12-inch knife and stabbed her through the abdomen, nailing her to the floor.

He stayed there, gawping at her corpse, listening to the radio for as long as it took to drink the bottle of whisky he'd brought with him. The more he drank, the more he contemplated suicide again. He pulled the bloody knife from her solar plexus and, for a second, thought about plunging it in his own. Then changed his mind and threw it into his bag.

Before letting himself out he folded her arms over her chest and closed her eyelids, as she might look laid out in her coffin, covering her body with clothes as a makeshift shroud. This is how the police discovered her 12 days later.

A full year almost passed, the Chelsea pensioner killer remains at large. The hands that murdered Isabella Griffith are still out there. Waiting to kill again. Hot blood pulsing through their guiltless veins.

Right now, warm and soapy, wiping plates and cutlery sticky with barbeque sauce in the kitchen of the Chicken Inn on Leicester Square. It's not where they want to be, and they won't be there for many days longer. They're in and out of work the way they are nuthouses, and their owner's been a diagnosed headcase since the age of 13.

Whatever his hands get up to, it's all *their* fault for not locking him up and throwing away the key. He's told them so. It even says it on his files. He has the makings of 'a cold psychopathic killer'. But then there's always some do-gooder on the board convinced he can be cured given the chance of a room in a probation hostel and another job with a dishcloth or a spade in his hands.

So here he is. A cold psychopathic killer washing his last pot, wiping his hands, collecting his coat and stepping out into the evening crowds pulling between *The Man with the Golden Gun* at the Odeon and *Earthquake* at the Empire. Anonymous and unaccosted.

If anyone sees him at all, they see just a thin young man taking the escalator down to the underground. Another quiet passenger sitting on the Northern Line staring blankly at his reflection in the window opposite: the gaunt wolverine face, the thick smileless lips, the cold dark eyes set in a brow like a fierce charcoaled V. Not what he sees gazing back at him as the carriage noisily shunts its way south.

Stand up and salute, you Schweinhunds! That's 'Franklin Bollvolt the First' you're looking at! A name to be feared and remembered like Hitler's!

The would-be Führer alights at Stockwell, emerging into dark lamplit streets of dark lamplit faces. The most dangerous borough in London, now that it's official you've more chance of being mugged in Lambeth than in New York City. The culprits, always, are West Indian. According to the *Evening News*, it's because they've nothing else to live for.

'To be young and black in London is to be without hope.'

Not as Franklin Bollvolt sees it through his Aryan scowl, headful of Messerschmitt engines, Panzer battalions and a million marching Brownshirts, picking up pace as he turns off towards his digs. Number 48 Grantham Road, where his surrogate family, the Cowdreys, rent him a room in their shabby terrace for £5 a week. Not that he uses it much, but it's somewhere to keep his books on fascism and the Third Reich, all borrowed from libraries and never returned, and his picture of Hitler, pinned on the wall above his bed the way other young men of 22 might have a topless Gillian Duxbury torn from the *Sun*.

His real treasures he hides beneath the floorboards. The spoils of his many crimes, including the mahogany cigarette box he stole from Isabella's house, and his pride and joy – a giant Nazi swastika which he spent hours gluing together from matchsticks.

Tonight, if there aren't any war films on the telly, he may just sit in his room and read about the SS. Or nip out for another cheap bottle of scotch. Get drunk. Get violent. Goosestep around the living room, barking in pidgin German, threatening to strangle Mrs Cowdrey. It wouldn't be the first time.

Because the urge hasn't left him. Sooner or later, his monster must be fed. It's like he says.

'Any man doing a killing enjoys it. It is an animal experience.'

Good evening, Patrick.

★

THE WEEKEND PASSES in fourth round cup ties, dashed hopes and drained tankards.

Friday, Angie throws a party in Oakley Street inviting friends to marvel at her pre-recorded interview with Russell Harty when it airs straight after the news and *Police 5*.

Saturday, Maggie attends the Finchley and Friern Barnet Conservative Association dinner dance where a camera crew from *World in Action* film her every foxtrot.

Sunday, Patrick is comatose on the sofa in 40 proof dreams of Kristallnacht as morning's light slowly soaks through the curtains in Grantham Road. The streets are quiet, save for the faint tread of the paper boy, plodding louder as his shoes flop directly outside the living-room window. But no papers today for the Cowdreys. The letterbox doesn't flap. Patrick doesn't stir. The boy's footsteps disappear.

Round the corner, his weighty satchel slowly lightening as he unloads the *People* and the *News of the World* down Kimberley Road, left onto Landor where he shoves a *Sunday Mirror* through the flap of 155, cutting down Dalywell where the *Sunday Times* thuds onto doormats, then turning into another street of densely packed three-storey terraces. The lighter his bag, the springier his step, as on he bounces, right past the gate of number 40 Stansfield Road. Not half a mile from where Patrick slumbers in final solutions – the house where David was born.

The house where his mother gave birth 28 years ago, no sooner out of her womb when the midwife turned to her and said something which at the time she found only a little unsettling. Today, it haunts her like some cursed prophecy.

'This child has been on this earth before.'

With lumbago backs and fluffy slippers, the paper boy's labours are swiped up, shaken and unfolded upon soft chairs and kitchen tables, dissected in grunt-punctuated silence and slurps from Ridgway teacups. The confessions of Ronnie Biggs' mistress. A police artist's impression of 'Public Enemy No. 1'. A London school teacher battered by a female pupil with a wooden club. Shocking scenes at yesterday's nil–nil draw between Leeds and Wimbledon where fans were stabbed in the arse and shot in the face with airguns.

'It throws a new dangerous light on soccer hooliganism.'

And tonight's television. Frank Sinatra live in concert at Madison Square Garden. A romantic comedy with Sidney Poitier. A documentary about Costa Rican turtles. And at five past ten, another *Omnibus* documentary on BBC One.

Cracked Actor.

Six miles away, in Albemarle Road Mrs Jones sits at the Bauhaus kitchen table David bought when he helped furnish her flat, the steam rising from her first cuppa of the day not as thick as the smoke from her second Embassy. Staring up at her, an article in this week's *Radio Times* she's already read too often since she bought it on Friday. But today is the day and she can't help but scan the same columns one more time.

'*David Bowie, the subject of this week's* Omnibus *film, is a twentieth-century phenomenon: rock star, ex-mime, visionary, self-confessed bisexual.*'

And one more time her nose wrinkles in distaste.

'*In the beginning there was no David Bowie, so he had to invent himself. He began as David Jones, son of a public relations man for Dr Barnardo's Homes.*'

She pauses, taking another drag.

A public relations man?

They couldn't even bother to name him. John, her late husband. Peggy gave David his eyes, his teeth and his music. John gave him everything else. David was always a daddy's boy, and five years after he helped her scatter John's ashes, he still is.

'*He may not be a great performer. But, even if the starlight is tinsel on plaster, he is, unquestionably, a star.*'

She sighs, flapping the magazine shut and glances at the clock. Still twelve hours to go.

The empty day is her jail sentence. She writes a letter, she dusts the bedroom, she makes a simple sandwich lunch and listens to *Family Favourites.*

A bath and a light supper help halve the distance till evening.

The television on, the tension building, Ol' Blue Eyes serenades her to quarter past eight. Magic tricks and a classical piano concert over on Two kill the last desperate hours until ten. She flicks over midway through the news with Richard Whitmore. Impatience eating her alive come the national weather forecast.

Then, on the stroke of 10.05, her David.

BOWIEODYSSEY75

The first glimpse of him is through two TV screens: her own and another in an American hotel room where he's being interviewed on KABC-TV's *Eyewitness News*. He looks like a skeleton wearing a Liberace wig, his limbs like saplings, his speech sniffy, abstract and contrary, his jaw sagging, dumb and open-mouthed. A jump cut, and he's suddenly a death mask, mortuary white and lifeless, his face being laboriously cast in layers of wet plaster until his head resembles a wasps' nest with a pair of nostrils. Minutes later, and he's now a shadow in black, face obscured by the rim of a fedora, acting very strangely in the back of a limousine, giggling about flies in his milk.

The cigarette in her fingers burns down to a drooping column of ash, the expression on her face more horror than wonder. Horror that *this* is her son. The child she was told had been on this earth before. The one whose records she sobs to every other evening. The reason she's stalked around the shops by strangers who want to see the woman who gave birth to this . . . *monster!*

'One isn't totally what one is conditioned to think.'

Good night, Peggy.

FOUR

IF HIS MOTHER COULD SEE HIM NOW. Workhouse thin, siloed eyes so wide, so still, they look like they've been painted on top of closed lids, blinking only when he siphons up the gunpowder blasting them back open. Her son does not look well, but nor does he necessarily look sick. He's far, far too handsome to pass for sick. Waxen and unreal, like Valentino laid out in his casket. Undeadly beautiful.

```
He grimaces. He takes deep breaths. He
walks with difficulty. But there is a
strong and determined look on his face. He
does not look like a man who will give up.
```

His eggshell attention strains on the script in his lap. The film his London talent agent wants him to make called *The Man Who Fell to Earth*. Miss Abbott flew over last week to deliver it by hand, only he was still too high on the song he'd recorded with John to take it in. She wanted to talk motion pictures. David just wanted to brainwash her with 'Fame' on repeat at gum-bleeding volume.

Miss Abbott's been one of the first to visit David's new home, not that it feels like one. After nine months of unpaid room service bills on Central Park he's taken rent of a three-storey house way down on West 20th Street between Seventh and Eighth. Pictures have been hung, cushions tossed, rugs unfurled and potted plants delicately arranged, but the unpacked packing cases still outnumber the furniture. The kitchen and dining room are in the basement, that much easier access for the rats and roaches, bare staircases connecting the floors above comprising small bedrooms, an office, a bathroom and his attic bedroom above the lounge where he now sits struggling to read past page one.

When Miss Abbott first came she found the house cold and uninviting. So did her friend, the very English director Mr Roeg who she brought over three nights later. They're right. It is. Unwelcomingly cold and eerily uninviting. A century ago it would have made a decently bleak opium den. A century on it still might as well be. This isn't a place someone would ever come to live, only to hide. Why David chose it.

He is a fugitive now. As of last week, when he ready-and-aimed at Defries, then fired with the squeeze of his new Beverly Hills lawyer, Mr Lippman.

The shot followed an emergency meeting in RCA's Sixth Avenue skyscraper with the division vice president and suited executives flown over from London. David turned up in bellbottoms and a beret looking like a sailor – a seasick one, his face the colour of a bad oyster.

It had all felt very different a week earlier in the white-beak heat of Electric Lady with a Beatle at his side, funking 'Fame' with Defries in its crosshairs. *'Bully for you!'* But come the crucial pow-wow in unforgiving daylight with men dressed like stockbrokers, David lost his bearings.

What saved him were the cards in his hand. So good he couldn't possibly lose however much his hands trembled as he lay them down.

His new album, *Young Americans*, is ready for release, now with extra tracks recorded with John Lennon. That trumped it in one. How could they say no to a man who'd brought them a Beatle? David had most of the masters safe in a bank vault, apart from the John tracks which Electric Lady would easily surrender for a slow wink and a fat backhander. In return, he begged RCA to cease channelling his money through Defries forthwith and pay him direct via Lippman, his new acting manager. He also requested a new office and a new car. They gave him the lot. Then, and only then, could David fire the gun.

The bullet was a sheet of headed notepaper from Lippman's Los Angeles legal firm of Cooper, Epstein, Hurewitz & Mark.

SIMON GODDARD

'On behalf of our client David Jones, AKA David Bowie, be advised that due to various violations of your agreements including but not limited to fraud in the inducement, all agreements with you and or any companies owned or controlled by you are hereby terminated effective forthwith . . .'

It ricocheted all the way uptown, from Mainman's Park Avenue office to Defries's penthouse on East 55th. But David knows, however deep the wound, it won't have been fatal. He's started a war, and that's what frightens him. The counterattack.

The house on West 20th is his military bunker. Only a handful of people know David lives here, and that doesn't include Defries. He'd never think to find him way down in Chelsea in this quiet brownstone no man's land of ornamental trees, rusting fire escapes and Puerto Rican turf wars. You walk down this block if you live here, if you're lost or to get somewhere else. The only regular footfall is the congregation of the Spanish Pentecostal church across the street, offering some comfort that if the worst comes to the worst, at least David's got God to protect him. And even if God should fail him, Corinne won't.

Corinne. Faithful as a lapdog, protective as a German Shepherd. Bombs may drop and bullets may fly. They won't get past Corinne. Nothing does. Hers is not flesh and blood but barbed wire and reinforced concrete, an insurmountable last defence between David and the outside world. His is now the war, but hers is the real mutiny. Defries's most-trusted general. That she could bite the hand that had fed and raised her from an office temp shaking out sacks of fan mail to the golden goose's protector in chief. Every task Defries ever gave her, Corinne executed brilliantly. Just a little too brilliantly. Her devotion was never to the job, only to David, and still is. Nothing has changed for Corinne, only the payer of her wages and her home address, now in a room of her own in West 20th to fulfil his every need with the same possessive monomania. Bar one.

The top job. Warmer of his bedsheets. Usually – but by no means exclusively – Ava, his lover, skinny as a pool cue with a head like an 8 ball sporting the shortest of dyed orange crops. And so Corinne makes the coffee while Ava drinks it under his covers. Corinne arranges the car while Ava snuggles in the back seat. Corinne sorts the tickets while Ava goes to the ball. Corinne stares sleeplessly at her bedroom ceiling while Ava screams in the attic. But when the screaming stops, Ava will fall asleep. Whereas Corinne keeps on staring. And thinking. And plotting.

So does David. It's the gunpowder kegging his brain, unable to sleep for the thoughts whizz-banging in his head like Chinese New Year, sixty explosions every minute of every day urging him to write, draw, paint or stick together strange gimcracks he's found in local junk shops to hang on his wall. Whatever he must do to elude the endless paranoias inaction brings. That he still isn't safe here. That Defries may already be bugging his phone. That he is in great danger from witches, warlocks and other psychic parasites intent on destroying him with spells, hexes and wickedest juju. That he must arm himself against them with whatever mystic hocus-pocus he can rally from his daunting library of occult literature. That soon he may have no choice but to leave this city. But go where? And do what? And be who?

NEWTON is alone. He is sitting on the ground in a hollow near the head of a disused mineshaft.

He rifles through the script in restless bursts, screwing up his nose, tossing it down again, unable to focus for the doodlebugs whistling between his ears. He still can't decide if he wants to play the doomed alien Thomas Newton, only that he's sick of playing the blessed rock'n'roll star David Bowie. But then he's already dead, or will be, just as soon as the glamless *Young Americans* hits the streets – scrubbed of make-up, shoes polished, casually dressed in belt and braces, the biggest betrayal of a fanbase since the Dodgers ditched Brooklyn for California. A soul record. By a man who no longer has one.

Outside, faint sirens howl and drips form icicles in the perishing Manhattan night. Inside, David racks out another thin white duke and his regal blitz continues.

He will still be sat there in the morning.

WHICH COMES TO NEW YORK in rubbed-out skies and flurries of snow shortening what's left of the city's patience to a car-honking trigger hair. And while the horns bark and breakfast griddles sizzle, in a rented studio flat a little further down West 20th Street, beneath a mop of short red curls another young English mind combusts with keen activity.

He came here to sell clothes, the ones he flew over with from his shop on the King's Road that's changed its name three times in as many years, each item labelled after the latest incarnation: 'SEX original'. But from the moment Malcolm signed the apartment lease he's spent most of his time, and money, on a rock'n'roll salvage mission. Never the plan, but in this city everyone's a mute extra until the streets hand them the script.

Malcolm was given his on West 23rd, the day he bumped into an old friend outside the Chelsea Hotel. He'd last seen Sylvain Sylvain in Paris at the end of '73, dodging French spit on stage with the New York Dolls. The look on Sylv's face said he wished he were still there. The Dolls were still together in name but in body only a last wheezing lurch from the knacker's yard. Their label had abandoned them after their second album flopped. So had their management. Two of them were now junkies and a third was an alcoholic. The best they can do is panhandle for gigs way out in Queens and Long Island while their former support band, KISS, pack out Uptown theatres with their greasepaint dunce-rock. What slim chance the world had given the Dolls they'd conclusively blown, now luckless innovators cursed to be forgotten in an age of gutless imitators.

This was the sorry tale Sylv told Malcolm. Any sorrier, it might have broken his heart. Instead, it lit a lightbulb.

A band. Not the first time he'd thought about it. The kids hanging round his King's Road shop are always nudging him. Glen, the Saturday boy from Saint Martin's art school, and his mates Steve and Paul, three flash young toerags desperate to be the next Faces and convinced they could be if only Malcolm would manage them. But they're just kids. Whereas the Dolls are five seasoned rock'n'roll mannequins ready for him to dress up and play with. They have the music. He has the clothes. Cases of them he's just flown over from London: stretch nylon, cire, rubber and leather, itching to be worn by the band with enough nerve. And Sylv's band have more than's ever been good for them.

Which is how, by a freak roll of Manhattan roulette, Malcolm now finds himself manager of the New York Dolls.

Putting his money where his mouth is, he's hired them a new rehearsal space, a loft right next door to the Chelsea. He's also covered their medical

BOWIEODYSSEY75

bills, finding a specialist doctor for the junkies, Johnny and Jerry, and a week's dry-out rehab for Arthur the alcoholic. As an image change, he stipulates new uniforms of made-to-measure 'SEX original' shiny scarlet vinyl shipped over from London, prompting Sylv and Johansen to write a new song, 'Red Patent Leather'. He also wants them to play their next gig in front of a Communist flag as a token of their new 'entente cordial' with the People's Republic of China. The Dolls can't think of any reason not to.

The morning snow falls softly outside Malcolm's window as his hand stretches across to his telephone. Right now it'll be just after lunch on the King's Road where he has urgent overseas business to report. He asks the operator to connect him long distance.

'Chelsea, three five one, zero seven six four.'

There follows a prolonged mechanical hiccup of ringing tones. It picks up with the background fuzzy '*bah-bah*' thump of the Troggs from the shop's jukebox. Then a voice he doesn't recognise.

'Hello, SEX.'

A young female voice, the accent South Coast, the attitude pressure-hosed by 19 years of *Swan Lake*, *Star Trek* and a slavish devotion to David Bowie. Must be a new girl they hired sometime since he flew over here.

'This is Malcolm,' he says. 'Who's that?'

And over the screaming hullaballoo of the Troggs she tells him.

'Jordan.'

SIXTY MILES NORTH OF 430 KING'S ROAD, from Malcolm's shop with its pink walls of situationist graffiti and chicken wire, from its ripped T-shirts, fetish masks and peek-toe plastic shoes, from its jukebox stuffed full of Vince Taylor, Joe Meek and the Troggs, from Jordan in her dyed blonde bouffant, plastic belt and tennis skirt, there is yet another monster.

He doesn't look like one, but then so few of them do. A little man in his little van, parked in a quiet grove in Cambridge, rolling up loose baccy from an old Allenburys Pastilles tin. In the back, cases of Graham's Malvedos and White Satin gin from Dolamore's cash and carry. In this town the dons do the thinking but he supplies their drinking. It pays enough, but then it's not all about the £27 a week. The perks are

SIMONGODDARD

priceless. Every day, roaming free in his four-wheeled key to the city. Nobody knows the streets of Cambridge better than he does. Every road, every back alley, every garden fence, every loose window, every Yale lock, every back door to every student hostel, every house sliced up into bedsits. And almost the names of every girl paying the rent.

Those he doesn't are easily found. See, he's a clever little monster. Reads the 'To Let' ads in the local paper to keep score on who's moving in and out. Spends spare afternoons in the library studying names and addresses on the electoral roll like an archaeologist poring over the Rosetta Stone. But that's just the background checks. The real work is reconnaissance, which is all the excuse rattling from campus to campus with a van full of pinot noir affords him. For an ex-lag he'd make a good copper. As good as his favourite, Lieutenant Kojak.

'Who loves ya, baby?'

Not his wife. Not the way he'd like. Twelve years younger than him, a plump and juicy 33 but dead from the waist down. After six years of marriage she'll sit and watch *Kojak* with him in their static caravan, 'Villa del Sol', but when he drags out the projector and his 8mm reels of *Splendid Night* and *Pussy Love* she doesn't want to know. Neither writhing on the screen nor reenacted between the sheets. Poor Margaret. None of this is her fault.

Even so.

It began last October, a few weeks after *Kojak* started on Saturday nights on BBC One. When the clocks turned back, and the nights drew in, and the burglars slithered out into the darkness like so many snails after a heavy rainfall. None more slithery than him, 5 foot 4 inches, scuttling over walls and rooftops like a trapeze artist. At the age of ten he could slip inside any house easy as breaking an egg. Borstal and prison didn't cure him. Nor did 18 months in Broadmoor, but then he never was your regular cat burglar. Otherwise, he'd be jemmying the sash windows over in Newnham, filling his swag bag with silver canteens and candelabras. Not fiddling the locks of dilapidated Victorian terraces in bedsit land, pilfering worthless knickknacks. Women's clothes, make-up, jewellery, tights, bras, wigs, falsies, plastic sunglasses. Booty he can't fence, but then he doesn't steal for cash but to stash – behind the workbench, under the floorboards in the shed behind his caravan. He can't stop himself but then as the saying goes, once a thief. Because that's all he ever was. Once.

BOWIEODYSSEY75

Until that Friday. The night before *Kojak*. A two-up, two-down in Mitcham's Corner, a quiet road, no through traffic, the curtains drawn and just a passage light on. He came in through the front door as easy as finding a key under the mat, then fused the lights. If there was anyone home, they'd now be plunged in darkness. There was, and he found her in one of the upstairs bedrooms, alone in just her dressing gown. He tied her hands behind her back and put a pillowcase over her head. She never saw his face. To her, he was just a shadowy brute force and a voice from hell.

'I came to rob you,' it said. 'But I think I'll rape you.'

When it was over he stole twelve quid in cash then left her tied up on the floor.

He didn't come home to his caravan until the early hours. Margaret was already in bed and never asked where he'd been. The next night they sat together watching *Kojak* as usual, waiting the best part of 20 minutes before Telly Savalas finally said the magic words.

'Who loves ya, baby?'

Two weeks later, he did it again. A house not half a mile from the first on the other side of the Cam. His 22-year-old victim was having a bath when he broke in, fused the lights, stuffed an ether pad over her mouth and threatened to kill her. Then he tied her up and did what monsters do.

The third was careless. Too soon, too rash, too greedy. A terrace opposite Fitzwilliam College, a Monday night during *Coronation Street*. He rang the doorbell, thinking he could frighten his way in wielding a kitchen knife, wrapped only in a blanket and wearing two wigs on top of one another as a disguise. The girl who answered kicked him in the balls, tore his top wig off and threw it after him as he scarpered. It was only luck that he managed to creep back and retrieve it before the police could bag it as evidence. *Stupid! Stupid! Stupid!* He'd never try that again, and two nights later a change of tactics found him raping a music student in the grounds of Homerton college.

So it continued.

All the way to Christmas. Two more break-in rapes, one victim suffering knife wounds to her arms as she failed to fight him off. He'd also started to make decent headlines in the local paper. Features on pages seven and nine which he cut out and glued inside an exercise book.

SIMONGODDARD

Fame!

Then the coppers called him in. Routine questioning of known ex-cons. His file had plenty of meat on its bones but he denied all knowledge. He also looked nothing like his discombobulated victims' fuzzy descriptions of a taller assailant.

A scare, but it didn't stop him. Just cautioned him enough to take time out. Even rapists need a Christmas holiday, and he spent his quietly at home, watching *Kojak*, blue films, forcing sex on frigid Margaret and masturbating furiously in his shed amongst his treasure trove of stolen femininity.

But now it's a new year. The Year of the Monster.

And so, back to work.

He finishes his roll-up, steps out, shutting and locking the driver's door with gloved hands, then walks purposefully towards a narrow gap between the terraces a hundred yards away. Reaching it, he slips down the passage leading onto the alley separating opposite backyards. His pace slows, halting by a low brick wall with a wooden gate. He pushes it. It doesn't move. He takes a step back, raises his arms, and with a gymnastic hop rolls his squat body over the brickwork into the yard.

He scuttles the short distance to the kitchen door. Slowly, he turns the handle.

Locked.

From his pocket he pulls a large ring of keys. He jiggles. A click. He tries again.

He's in.

He treads silently over cracked lino into the corridor. At the far end, the front door with today's letters waiting to be collected from the hessian mat. A reassuring sign the coast is clear.

He bends down and picks them up. The bills he drops. The handwritten envelopes he inspects one by one. He's become a good amateur calligraphist. Something about a parent's writing he can always tell. Those, he discards. But this one, the way the t's are crossed. He has a hunch this is someone's boyfriend. Vital private information he can read later. Something to torture her with in the depths of her pitch-black horror when he'll ask whether so-and-so 'did it like this?' He stuffs it inside his pocket and turns up the staircase.

33

BOWIEODYSSEY75

The cream paintwork of its walls chipped and flaking. There are pairs of knickers drying over the top banister. They stop him in his tracks, just a moment, to linger and look, resisting the urge to touch.

Over thin threadbare carpet he crosses the landing and carefully pushes open a bedroom door. He pokes his eye round. Empty. He steps inside.

He stares at the single bed in the corner. He can reach it in three, maybe four steps and have his knife at their throat before they knows he's there.

He creeps softly to the wardrobe. He already knows from the make-up on the dressing table and the faint musky perfume but it's always good to check. Nothing like the shock of a rail of men's shirts to thwart his plans. But, as he thought, soft hanging fabrics, the tips of his glove stroking along their edges.

Beside it, a chest of drawers. He pulls open the top. Always, the top. The underwear drawer. He gently pokes between whites, greys and pinks until pinching a thin strip of black and teasing it out. Rubbing it between his fingertips, he can feel the silkiness even through his gloves. He dangles it in the air, the light catching the material's sheen. Then, closing his eyes, presses it hard against his face, sucking in the air like an oxygen mask. Opening them, he wipes it across his lips before stuffing it in a pocket with one hand and closing the drawer with his other.

His eyes twitching, he picks up a lipstick, reads it, puts it down again. He pokes a finger in an open trinket box that can't be shut for all the beads, bangles and necklaces piling high above its edges. The paperback books – a selection of blue Pelicans including *The Future of the Social Services*, some Brontës and *Jonathan Livingston Seagull* – he ignores. Same as the cassettes piled up beside a Carousel radio and tape machine, a mix of Scotch C60s with handwritten inlays – '*Beatles Pepper*', '*Tubular Bells etc*' – and half a dozen bought ones including *Dark Side Of The Moon*, *Ziggy Stardust* and *Diamond Dogs*.

Backing towards the door, he turns and takes a last mental Polaroid of the layout, glancing at the pictures above the bed. Souvenirs of student demos. 'KEVIN GATELY WAS KILLED'. A psychedelic zodiac. Postcards by Mucha and Klimt. And a recent colour pin-up from *Sounds* of a man on stage in America wearing dark glasses with a cloak draped across his shoulders.

He doesn't even read the name. 'David Bowie'. Just stands there, pockets bulging with skeleton keys, stolen panties and a letter from someone's boyfriend, eyes glazing at the scene of his future crime. Knowing that when he returns, everything will be perfect.

'Who . . .

      . . . loves . . .

            . . . ya . . .

                  . . . baby?'

FIVE

THE NEW YORK OF *KOJAK* IS NOTHING LIKE THE REAL CITY. For one, it's mostly filmed in Los Angeles. For another, its fictional streets are crowded with junkies, prostitutes, crooked cops, drug smugglers, stranglers, stabbers and psychopathic bombers. The real New York isn't nearly so safe.

From way up in Lexington down to the Village, stores are now opening for business by locking their front doors. After five knives at their throats in as many months, some owners are becoming a little choosier who crosses their threshold. No blacks, no Hispanics, no single men of any colour, however well dressed. Potential customers must stand outside on the other side of the glass and wait to be assessed by nervous cashiers who can't help but see the Norman Bates in everyone. Takings are abysmal, but rapid insolvency is now the price of an unsliced jugular vein in a city where daylight robbery is as common as bird shit.

Those who make it home safely every day without being mugged, shot, raped or razored can remind themselves what they've missed as soon as they switch on their TV. Monday, repeats of *Ironside*. Tuesday, *Police Story* and *Barnaby Jones*. Wednesday, *Cannon*. Thursday, *The Streets of San Francisco* and *Harry-O*. Friday, *Baretta*, *Police Woman*, and for light relief, *The Rockford Files*. Saturday, there'll be a crime movie, new or old, somewhere on some channel, be it *Call Northside 777* or *Killers Three*. Sunday, either a *Columbo*, *McMillan & Wife* or *Amy Prentiss* and, always, a *Kojak*. Every day, on every screen and every street, the gunshots pitter patter like a ceaseless rain. The sound of New York, 1975.

There are others. Linda Ronstadt whines wearily at number 1, but the legs of this city prefer to keep syncopated stride with number 2. The Average White Band's 'Pick Up The Pieces' was written by Scotsmen and recorded in Miami but still makes a better theme for modern Gotham than the one from *Kojak*. Music danced to by the kind of people shop owners wouldn't unlock their doors for. The young, the gay, the Latino and the black. Every weekend, from Le Jardin on Times Square to the Flamingo in SoHo, their hungry bones throb to Herbie Mann hijacking their love, the clavinet boogie of Jimmy Castor and the railroad funk of B.T. Express. By comparison, everything else on the radio is an acid reflux of yesterday. The bliss of disco is that it feels forever now.

The only tomorrow people can be found down on the Bowery. CBGB's undersells itself as 'The New Place For Music', wasting 'New' on the wrong noun. You can still hear the past in Blondie and Television but both try their hardest to punch their way out of it. The latter threaten the most likely knockouts. In the distorted echo of a half-empty cave, 'Blank Generation' and 'Marquee Moon' don't yet sound too good for today, but give it a year and they will do. This coming Saturday they play here again on the same bill as CBGB's debutante Patti Smith. By Sunday, tomorrow should feel a whole lot closer.

Up on 23rd Street, it couldn't be further away. In Malcolm's hired loft, the Dolls are keenly tunnelling escape routes back to 1972. New labours like 'Teenage News' help remind them who they once were but don't change who they still are, which is old musketeers. The only forward motion comes from their pin-cushion-armed D'Artagnan, Johnny Thunders, whose 'Pirate Love' sounds like it might yet still be drinkable if left in the back of his fridge until 1977. They will doubtless dazzle flying the hammer and sickle in their new red leatherette but musically, deep down, even Malcolm must know the Dolls are just mutton dressed as Mao.

Beyond the wild rumbles from the Bowery, Seventies rock'n'roll is a clogged artery. If medical evidence were ever needed, tonight its principal monsters of saturated fat drip all over the stage of Madison Square Garden. Much like the Dolls, Led Zeppelin sound exactly as they did three years

BOWIEODYSSEY75

ago and rely on the amplified squeals of a functioning heroin addict. There, the similarity ends. The Zep started the decade at number 1 in the US and five years later nothing has changed. New York loves them enough to sell out three nights at the Garden, but then New York is a town which daily flushes its bodyweight in frankfurters. The Zep are white bun rock'n'roll, with or without onions – bare chests, *'baby, baby'*, double-neck guitars and drum solos stretching longer than most geologic periods of the Mesozoic era. Inside the Garden it may as well still be 1971. Even the joints smell the same. But then nobody walks into a Zep gig expecting the shock of the new.

That includes David, watching with Ava from the VIP huddle of the wings, dressed like a withered Jack Nicholson from *Chinatown* – unbelted slacks, jacket, fat tie, a backwards tilting fedora and impenetrable dark glasses that make his face look even more like a skull than it does without them.

He's here by special invite. Six nights ago, David found himself in the Zep's suite at the Plaza surrounded by young girls, stoned journalists, pills, powder, bourbon, the latest jazz fusion from Alphonse Mouzon and fractured memories of ten years earlier. Back in the days of in-and-out sessions on the clock in Portland Place, where everyone knew everyone but nobody knew which of them would one day become David Bowie and Jimmy Page. When David was still a Manish Boy and Jimmy not yet a Yardbird, their futures unwritten and their souls still for sale.

In the Garden, it looks and sounds to David like Jimmy sold his to the higher bidder. The curved cyclorama backdrop and 300 kilowatts of lighting effects, all synchronised by a mini-computer including a Krypton laser entombing Jimmy in a green three-dimensional pyramid. The Zep may sound as advanced as their nineteenth-century airship namesake but they've transformed their stage into Spacecraft Discovery One.

David is spellbound. By the strobes, the lasers, the puffs of smoke, the atomic machismo, the spotlit preening, the pompous virtuosity, the hubristic absurdity, the high-cholesterol fuckerocity of it all. It's like some sterile fascist mindtrick to bullwhip the pliant masses into unthinking submission. A Nuremberg rally disguised as the Bath Blues Festival. Just look at it. Twenty thousand kids, some of whom got teargassed in the riot for tickets, all deafened and dumbstruck by the hag-like squalls of

38

'the Best Chest in Rock' and the diabolical scrapes of a violin bow against 24,000 watts of amplified Les Paul.

This isn't rock'n'roll. This is *evil*. David can see it, can hear it. So awesome, so *awful*, this has to be the Devil's music.

A prickly chill creeps over him.

The Devil's music?

What the literal hell has Jimmy done to make it?

BENEATH THE DRAB LOTHIAN SKY, the council flats are full of dreamers. Gums burning from Cola Cubes, nails chewed, skin mutton-pied, greasy fingers turning the pages so fast they risk ripping them.

'Ooh, Alan!'

The auld one. Five feet ten. Left-handed son of an undertaker. Brushes his teeth with Pearl Drops. Likes Led Zeppelin, *The Goodies*, Jensen Interceptor cars and dark rum and peppermint. Dislikes pushy girls and cruelty to animals.

'Ooh, Derek!'

The blond one. Five feet ten. Alan's wee brother. Smiles like he was born with twice the amount of teeth he should have and brushes them with Pearl Drops. Likes his dog called Jamie, goldfish, the Carpenters and making extra-hot curries served with sultanas and bananas. Has worn a crucifix round his neck since the age of 12.

'Ooh, Eric!'

The dopey blue-eyed one. Five feet nine. Decorates himself in smiley and *love is . . .* badges. Brushes his teeth with Signal. Likes Yes, *The Lord of the Rings*, Barbra Streisand films and peach flambé. Scared of drowning.

'Ooh, Woody!'

The bairn. A peely-wally five feet eight. Says he believes in ghosts. Also brushes his teeth with Pearl Drops. Likes steak and chips, Bugs Bunny, Neil Sedaka and his mother's white pudding. Hates pizza.

'Ooh, Les!'

The dreamy one. Five feet nine. Spends his spare time quietly reading *Chariot of the Gods* wondering if God was really an astronaut. No preference for toothpaste brand specified. Likes cars, films about cars including *Vanishing Point*, the colour blue, Sugar Puffs and his mother's tattie soup. Hates drainpipe troosers.

'OOH, ROLLERS!'

Their eyes like kittens, bedazzled by bright reds criss-crossed with whites and blacks hemming cuffs and collars and half-mast breeks. And so long as they keep mooning at the shoo-be-doo faces, the sha-la-la teeth, the gonky hair and the stripy socks, they'll keep on dreaming. Because as soon as they stop and look outside their window and see nothing but an infinity of stratus clouds hanging like loft insulation suffocating the skyline, those dreams will pop quicker than their next pink Bubbly.

Somewhere far above that impenetrable greyness, not that anyone looking up would see it, a plane fast approaches from the south. Tens of thousands of feet above the same dream-starved streets the Bay City Rollers escaped from, starting its descent just before the low roofs of Gilmerton, still invisible above the sandstone tenements of Dalry, barely a shadow in the sky over the schemes of Broomhouse, its engines screeching louder, its landing gear dropping as it plummets ever closer to the runway until the Hawker Siddeley Trident with its British Airways tailfin touches down smooth as a heron. The stairs are wheeled into place, the door opens and a waving figure emerges to applause, cheers, flashbulbs and a kilted piper playing a traditional air by Rabbie Burns.

'A Man's A Man For A' That'.

She sure is. Even with her handbag. The most famous man in the country. For a' that.

Fame. It's a new sensation for Maggie. Not the cameras and the microphones poking in her face. That she's long used to like any other politician. It's *the way* they're poking, and the fever in the eyes of the people who poke them. The same fever in the eyes of the party faithful gaping at her now, the chairwomen of a Scottish Tory Advisory Committee trembling as she pins a welcome sprig of lucky white heather to the right lapel of Maggie's Donegal tweed suit.

And I dared to touch the chosen one!

A look of love, awe and willing servitude that could make anyone headbutting-drunk with power.

Maggie could get used to it.

The cork popped last week when she became the first woman in human history to be elected leader of a political party. An impossible feat achieved, in part, with the help of her campaign manager, a former Colditz escapee evidently used to performing miracles. Overnight she went from 'Margaret' the MP of parliamentary headlines to 'Maggie' the tabloid superstar. A household name and face more instantly recognisable than most of the acts in the Top 10 bar Donny and Marie Osmond.

Those for her, like the *Daily Mail*, hail her *'a one-woman revolution'*. Those against, like the *Mirror*, still concede she is now *'the most powerful woman politician in the Western world'*. And the most famous.

So far this week she's had breakfast at Claridge's with Henry Kissinger and spent a lovely lunchtime with her friend Jimmy Young on Radio 2, where between the soothing sounds of Andy Williams and the Cascading Strings both agreed they loathed the word 'class'.

Yesterday, she formally accepted the Tory leadership before a mass gathering of True-Bluers in the Europa Hotel on Grosvenor Square. It's on the front of this morning's *Sun* under the headline 'CORONATION DAY!' with Maggie's face many times bigger than that of Angie Bowie, tucked in the top right corner as a secondary sell. Like any other stock market, fame is a numbers game measured in sizes, and as of the second week in February her shares are skyrocketing. More famous than Mrs Bowie, than Ben from the beefburger ads, than Steve Harley and Cockney Rebel. Come up and see her, make Maggie smile.

Scotland does. Contorting her lips in strange new gurnings of giddy delirium. After a courtesy press conference she is whisked to the heart of Edinburgh for a scheduled walkabout to 'meet the people' in the St James shopping centre. Sensible conversations with local housewives and, if time, the chance to pick up some shortbread for Denis. That's what Maggie expects.

Not Rollermania.

Fans. *Hundreds* of them, pushing, shoving, treading on toes, so many that within seconds she can no longer move forwards or back. Most of them women, young and old, desperate to see not the Tory leader, not Mrs Thatcher, but 'Maggie'. One name, one fame.

Her oot the papers and aff the news. Maggie, ken that blonde wifey with the handbag? Aye, that Maggie! And a braw name it is too. Just like Maggie frae The Broons. *Oor Maggie! Your Maggie! A'body's Maggie!*

Every one of them clamouring for her signature, on their shopping list, on their betting slip, on the casts of their broken limbs. Heaving, swaying, elbowing, stumbling, just to touch, smell and hear her speak.

'Aw, she's a luvvely woman,' sighs a bent-up pensioner stuck at the rear, 'only I wish she was a wee bitty taller.'

An avalanche of faces, everywhere she turns. Someone tosses her a tartan hat. A man's voice yells 'Welcome tae Scotland!' A stray hand thrusts a box of Edinburgh Rock at her. 'A wee souvenir for ye, Maggie!' One woman sways and faints. Others trapped in the crush start to cry.

Maggie keeps smiling, waving royally. 'Is everyone all right back there?' she asks. 'One really *would* like to buy some shortbread.'

But her battered twelve-strong security detail have seen enough. Encircling her like a rugby scrum, panting and straining, they back her into the nearest shop, McGowan's the jewellers, and lock the door.

A man from Special Branch asks her if she's alright.

'I'm fine,' grins Maggie, exhilaration bubbling in her cheeks.

The shop window shudders, bodies squashing against the outside glass as if trapped under a microscope slide. Just like the ones Maggie used to scrutinise as an Oxford chemistry graduate working for J. Lyons & Co. She tilts her head, gazing at them dreamily. All these queer little particles of squirming humanity suddenly at her disposal.

Later, after her rapturous sausage-roll luncheon in the Assembly Rooms with 600 party officials, after the Tory Ladies of the Borders present her with a blue cashmere twinset, after she is whisked to Glasgow in a white Jaguar to be greeted by similar scenes in George Square, after addressing another 1,800 in a packed City Hall to rafter-cracking cheers, banners of 'Wilson can't match her – win with Thatcher' and a chorus line of six Young Conservatives in lettered T-shirts together spelling out M-A-G-G-I-E, the press will ask Maggie for her reaction.

'This is the most marvellous welcome that any politician could ever have been given anywhere in the world,' she'll begin. Then they'll press her on how she feels, to be *this* loved, to be *this* famous. And Maggie's basilisk eyes will sparkle as she gleefully tells them.

'Fantastic!'

Fame is. As only the Bay City Rollers would tell her if they weren't currently 350 miles away on a Hampshire health farm recovering from

SIMON GODDARD

'nervous exhaustion'. While in the council flats beneath those drab Lothian skies, the tartan-jammied dreamers keep on dreaming.

GOOD OLD RON. If he doesn't know where the party is, that can only mean there isn't one. But he does. Always. He's got a nose for it. *The* nose for it, like a raven's beak. You're born with a nose like that, it'd be an insult to nature to waste it and Ron knows he's been blessed with a twin-cylinder vacuum cleaner bolted onto the centre of his face. Born to hoover. Why he always knows where the party is.

Tonight it's a 20-mile drive from the stage he's just stumbled off as the cherry on the cake of a three-hour Led Zeppelin gig. Ron joined them as their surprise guest for the final encore. Seven minutes of electric stink and now his day's work is done and his nose is twitching. So is his mate Jimmy's, only his can't pick up where the party is. That's why good old Ron is here.

Their driver goes where the nose tells him to. East out of Uniondale, back towards the city on the Long Island Expressway, through the Queens-Midtown tunnel, straight along 37th, left onto Fifth, down past the Empire State, on beyond the Flatiron, turning right into Chelsea until pulling up at the kerb in front of a dark three-storey terrace on West 20th.

David's house.

Where the party is.

Its life and soul is a large quantity of Titanium white powder just delivered from Los Angeles, now being heaped onto plates in the upstairs lounge of Ron's dear pal. 'David's cool, man,' he assures Jimmy, who doesn't know him nearly so well. Not that he cares. So long as it's where the party is.

A very intimate party. Just David, his girlfriend Ava and their LA friend Freddie. Everyone's friend Freddie, a Polish Jew who survived the Holocaust and has been celebrating ever since by advocating the joie de vivre of heavy narcotics including the generous heap which has Ron's snitch jiggling like Samantha's from *Bewitched* before he's halfway up the stairs. Just as he promised Jimmy. 'David's cool, man.'

He doesn't necessarily look it. Not to Jimmy, at least. David hasn't been right since the moment he saw Jimmy walk through the door when his face contorted like a Notre-Dame gargoyle. Still, there's the party, all piled up and waiting for everyone to tuck in. Ron's doesn't need telling twice. Down he goes, double barrels blazing. 'David's cool, man.'

So's the party. Grade A Merck, the five star pharmaceutical real deal manufactured in New Jersey for strictly-controlled medical purposes, so much purer than the gritty South American stuff. So pure Ron takes no notice of the spooky rhubarb striking up between David and Jimmy, catching only the occasional word as he divebombs for seconds. Something about Aleister Crowley, demons, Loch Ness and secret gateways to the bowels of Hell. But it's only rock'n'roll, assumes Ron. It's only ever rock'n'roll. Because 'David's cool, man'.

And Ron genuinely believes it. Even ten minutes later when he's back outside on the street with Jimmy, his snout sorely missing the party already. All because David suddenly flipped over a wine stain on one of his cushions.

It was the queerest thing. One second all was powder and paradise. The next, David was shrieking like a man who'd just seen some indescribable liquescent horror, gibbering about 'evil' and demanding Jimmy jump out of his window. When the pair of them decided to leave, opting for the stairs instead.

'Honestly, I don't know what the fuck's got into him,' sighs Ron, hailing their driver from across the street. 'He's never normally like that.'

Beside him, Jimmy says nothing, an odd faraway look in his black marble eyes, quiet as a dawn mist rolling across the shores of a Scottish loch where the monsters swim and the goblins softly rattle hidden gateways to Hell.

'Honestly,' repeats Ron, more confused than annoyed. 'David's cool, man.'

SIX

THE CUSHION DRIES BUT THE STAIN REMAINS. A stain much bigger than Jimmy's blotch of wine like half a Rorschach test, this one seeping through the couch, soaking the rug, dribbling through the floorboards, spreading up the walls, discolouring the pictures, poisoning the plants, oozing out onto the landing, dripping down the staircase, saturating every surface from the attic to the basement, polluting the whole house with its ungodly venom. David sees its contagion in everything he touches, souring the milk in his fridge, drenching the sheets on his bed, smearing the glass of his mirror and corroding the reflection within. A cruel contaminated likeness staring back at him in a black woollen tuxedo with wide satin lapels, matching hat, crisp dress shirt and bow tie. The facial membrane is still David Bowie but its tailored graces and pitiless detachment that of an English aristocrat from the 1930s, the kind who dined with the Mitfords, marched with Mosley and sided with Hitler; some depraved Kentish viscount who whips his servants and sneers at the poor from the rear of his chauffeur-driven Phantom II as he fritters his inheritance on laudanum and wenching. This is what David sees. This is what David has become.

A handsome ghoul in the rear of his own chauffeur-driven limo, drifting up Eighth Avenue through Sunday evening traffic, a strapless leather bag clutched in his lap and its contents already tautening his senses

BOWIEODYSSEY75

to piano wire. He looks without feeling at the city streaking past beyond his window. Bars, drugstores, luncheonettes, whites, blacks, Latinos, Chinese, playfighting kids, hand-clasping couples, jaywalking bums, heavy-coated old ladies staggering with brown paper grocery bags, all seven ages of man in an uninterrupted sidewalk carpet unrolling before his tempered glass eyeballs. Until the corner of 50th where his driver swerves right, circles a block and slows to a halt beside the mounted police barricades flanking the entrance to the Uris Theatre.

He is not immediately recognised since a fleshless wraith in a fedora and dinner suit is not recognisably anyone's idea of David Bowie. Not a stitch of him hollers rock'n'roll despite being here upon the invitation of rock'n'roll's annual knighting ceremony. The dress code for the seventeenth Grammy Awards specified black tie. David's is white, making his pallor seem only a fraction less sallow by contrast. Others have bent the rules as best they can: Stevie Wonder is in funky powder blue, Art Garfunkel in a long-sleeved jersey with mock bow tie and tux printed on top and Bette Midler wears a seven-inch single by the Del-Vikings as a hat.

David swoops between them seeking a comforting face and finds one in John – a Che Guevara beret on his head, a 'Dr Winston O'Boogie' medallion round his neck, a diamante Elvis brooch on his lapel and a rekindled Yoko on his arm. A different John to the one that cut 'Fame' six weeks ago, no longer living next door to Greta Garbo with a girl called May and two cats named Major and Minor but back with the wife in the same apartment block where they shot *Rosemary's Baby*. Just as David is a different David. Then, still just about human. Now, fully Count Dracula.

'He is, of course, David Bowie.'

Or so Andy Williams still seems to believe, introducing him to the Uris stage and the CBS television cameras broadcasting live. David enters minus his hat, a colourless matchstick man but for his torch of orange hair with flickers of blonde. He pauses twice to take a bow on his way to the lectern, when he gets there speaking in the measured bursts of a struggling United Nations translator, his sentences fractured by sudden dropout in his brainwaves' transmission. He sniffs tightly and theatrically; should anyone be in any doubt as to why, he makes a confessional pun emphasising the 'gram' in 'Grammy'. The audience laugh nervously. David raises a fist and leers.

He is, of course, completely mad.

Babbling in schoolboy French about 'ze premiere femme noir' he finally reminds himself and the audience why he's there, to present the award for the Best R&B Vocal Performance by a female artist. He reads out the nominees in turn, cryptically mispronouncing Etta James' 'St Louis Blues' as 'St Louis Blows', before unsealing the envelope, making a pantomime of fumbling in his pocket for reading glasses only to place a pair of tinted shades on his face. The audience still don't get him but just about get the gag as he announces this year's recipient. To his visible delight, his personal favourite.

'Miss Aretha Franklin.'

Whisked stagewards on a cyclone of applause, as the winner of the same category seven years running, the Queen of Soul doesn't look especially surprised. Only amused by what greets her. David hands over her miniature gold-plated gramophone, landing the ghostliest of pecks on her right cheek. Aretha, smiling, turns to the audience.

'Thank you,' she says, cradling her award in both hands. 'Why, this is so good I could kiss David Bowie.'

And the stake plunged through the vampire's heart turning his bones to dust.

IN THE DRUGGED AND DRUNKEN post-show pits below the Uris, David trips and stumbles, spilling the drink his feverish brain could ill withstand down the front of a woman's dress. Just as Jimmy did to his sacred silk cushion, the stained now the stainer, and he doesn't even notice. Not with eyes drowning in so much starry vomit. Braying monsters in their gold-sequined dresses, velvet waistcoats and diamond-studded cufflinks, those who haven't trophies smiling their gummiest smile lest anyone should see they'd sooner thrust sewing scissors into the greasy faces of those who have. And everyone spinelessly pretending that Grammy knows best: that the Song of the Year is 'The Way We Were' and not 'Sweet Thing'; that the Best Opera Recording is *La Boheme* and not 'Chant Of The Ever Circling Skeletal Family'; that the Album of the Year is *Fulfillingness' First Finale* and not *Diamond Dogs*; that the Best Male Pop Vocal Performer is Stevie Wonder and not David Bowie. Tin cups for the tin soldiers of Tin Pan Alley.

BOWIEODYSSEY75

He returns to West 20th Street as a patient to his sick bed after a limp round the hospital garden. A stained house in a stained city that will never be cleansed no matter how hard the spring rains flush out the gutters.

So long as he stays in it, nor will David, a foreign prisoner of its rock'n'roll high society. Of having always to act 'Bowie', one of *them*, seen among the to-be-seen and quarry of flash photography, being watched side of stage watching the Zep, watching Roxy, watching the Faces, swigging Blue Nun backstage with Rod, 'Ain't we geezers done good!', cadging cigs and 'Not 'arf!', a friend of John, a friend of Ron, a friend of Jagger, a friend of anyone as famous as he is and many that are more so, top of their guest lists, client of their dealers, sharer of their women, bloodsucker of their greatest hits. Just another cardboard character in a toy theatre dancing to the script of next week's *NME* 'Thrills' column.

The disappearing act of his new soul album, *Young Americans*, won't rescue him either, not that David has any intention to tour or promote it. His record company have just rush-released it in the States, swatting off judicial sabre rattling from Defries whose warpath gathers violent speed, furiously denying rumours of any managerial split in the papers as he rapid-fires cluster bombs of legalese without discrimination: at David, at RCA, at the ink ribbon in his telex machine every time it spews another ultimatum from some heinous solicitor in Beverly Hills. But his attempted injunction lands on their desk only after the first 200,000 copies of *Young Americans* have already shipped. It'll chart next week at number 84. In another month it will peak at 9, lagging behind John's ragbag rock'n'roll covers album, Bob Dylan, John Denver, Olivia Newton-John and the new double diplodocus from the Zep. Thirty-three and a third capitulations per minute.

A small Top 10 victory for David amid a losing battle. He can feel Defries on his skin like the static of an approaching electrical storm, part of the same stain, the unbreakable voodoo curse upon the house of Bowie, ringmaster of the suffocating evil now diseasing his every breath. There are over seven million people in New York City but this town ain't big enough for the both of them any longer. Defries is an enemy too far and 35 blocks too close. Why David has no choice but to take flight. By falling to earth.

His only means of escape – Thomas Newton.

Mr Roeg wants to start filming as soon as he can finalise the budget. David still doesn't like the script but he likes the character. More than the cardboard rock'n'roll star. More than the pale possessed fiend ogling back from his mirror. His logic – incinerated though it is by a forest fire of coca plants – that by pretending to be 'Newton', a lonely extraterrestrial billions of light years away from home, he can purge himself of everything that is 'Bowie'. Dropping one act by taking up another in the vain hope that in the transition between he may yet recover who the real 'David' is. Turning his back on the fetid music business by silencing the song and dance man. Locking the recording artist in his trunk like a ventriloquist's dummy and throwing away the key. A new career in a new town.

David Bowie – *Movie Star!*

And there's only one town where the movie stars go.

It lies at the end of two and a half thousand miles of rail track which will take him the best part of three days to get there. When he does, he won't have anywhere to live, only friends he can crash with, women he can sleep with and Freddie the dealer's phone number which'll keep his nostrils harried in the quantities to which they've long suffered with increasingly bloody consequences. He will travel alone on a one-way ticket, here today gone tomorrow, as clean a break as Ava's heart when he tells her she won't be going with him. Which silver-lines the cloud for Corinne when she realises neither will she, entrusted to stay and pack up the rest of his things on the assurance of joining him in California once he's settled. This departure must be made alone.

He carries with him only the absolute essentials: clothes, shoes and enough nasal irritant for a 72-hour train journey; his hundreds of books on everything from Nazi pseudoscience, Rosicrucian mysticism and ancient theosophy to the Great Pyramids, Kabbalah and psychic self-defence techniques; his scribbled-on script of *The Man Who Fell to Earth*; his sketchbooks and notepads full of his own unfilmable movie plots and storyboards; and the first scraps of a novel he's been toying with. A sort of memoir, or would be if only its author knew who he was beyond the cold mirror image of a would-be romantic with no emotion at all. So far, just a loose series of disjointed flashbacks and unhinged flashforwards between schoolboy reminiscences of grey flannel trousers, a graphic contemporary sex diary and snorted gobbledygook about divine witches and eternal damnation. A book as yet with no plot, no publisher and no ending in sight. Just a title.

The Return of the Thin White Duke.

SEVEN

SHE COULD HAVE WORN HER MINK but she thought it'd be too showy. As Peggy weighed it up, this wasn't a night at the Royal Variety Performance, only a day out with her daughter-in-law at the Ideal Home Exhibition, the tickets a mere 65 pence. Nice though it was for Angie to invite her.

'YOU'RE NOT WEARING YOUR MINK!'

And just like Angie to turn up in her own.

'STILL! DON'T *YOU* LOOK FAAABULOUS!'

Peggy, church smart in her winter coat with her hair washed and set, squeezes a smile as she would a near-empty tube of toothpaste. It's the first time she's seen 'Angela' this year: her hair back to its natural brown, medium cut and curled away from the face like the sort of Fifties film star who, indeed, would have worn her furs to water the house plants; her eyes blazing with breakneck energy just a few watts dim of certifiable mania; her mouth yet unable to drop its pitch below that of a tannoy on a sinking ship.

'OH! . . . NOW! . . . LOOK! . . . AT! . . . *THIS!*'

They stand on the entrance platform overlooking Olympia's Grand Hall, the entire ceiling canopy lined with muslin. A deliberately blank sky to focus all attention on the splendour beneath: a double-glazed fairyland of middle-class aspiration, Xanadus of tufted shag and wall cavity insulation,

BOWIEODYSSEY75

a model village for life-sized humans fortressed by a Georgian walled garden stretching the whole perimeter, at its centre a giant fountain giddily outspurting those in Trafalgar Square. And for a second even Peggy stops thinking about her son long enough to drink it in. But only a second.

Angie is not her David, but if it's answers Peggy's after, then she's a better bet than her cold telephone receiver. She knows her interrogation must be gently paced. Nothing hysterical, nothing judgemental, treading carefully lest they should revert to the bad old days of five years ago when she and Angie were forever 'having words'. It's now been an age of mutual truce since they last 'had words' but a slip of her tongue or one of her looks – the sort that would wrinkle the skin on a custard – and she knows similar words, or worse, could easily be had again. Patience, Peggy. Patience.

Descending to the main floor, they join the crowds milling along the miles of stalls: women in saris pouring cups of Indian tea, a Smithfield butcher in his straw boater dressing a saddle of lamb with kidneys, a vegetable patch encouraging the cash-strapped to transform their gardens into a self-sufficient larder, home sauna demonstrations and the latest electrical labour-saving devices from Rumbelows. Then the queues threading in and out of the show houses: the timber-framed, the bungalowed and the split-levelled, cooing over patio doors, serving hatches, en-suite bathrooms, the latest in Sony Trinitron TVs, crushed-ice dispensers and hidden ironing boards that plop like rabbits out of magicians' hats at the gentlest tap of a cupboard door. Other rooms made from waste materials, armchairs constructed from drainpipes, oil drums transformed into book cases, settees of compressed cardboard and a candelabra fashioned from paper cups. And all the while Angie casually klaxoning the latest headlines from Oakley Street.

'EVERY TIME HE FARTS I HAVE TO SEND HIM OUT OF THE ROOM!'

He being her new dog Marcus, a Dobermann Pinscher with a chronic wind problem and only one testicle.

'I HAVEN'T DECIDED WHAT I'LL SAY YET, BUT I WON'T LET THE BOYS DOWN!'

The boys being the black tailcoats of Eton College whose Contemporary Arts Society have invited Angie to present a guest lecture on the entertainment business later this month.

'IT'S GOT EVERYTHING. MYSTERY! GLAMOUR! SEX! DRAMA!'

It being the film about Ruth Ellis, made by the same director as *A Day in the Death of Joe Egg* in which she'll play the tragic lead, going into production just as soon as they gain the consent of the Ellis family.

'AND ISN'T *THIS* FAAABULOUS!'

This being the colonnaded entrance of another show house where Peggy follows Angie through into a living room so overwhelmingly beige it's like drowning in a cup of Mellow Birds. The only respite is the silver finish of the state-of-the-art Tandberg hi-fi system in the white polyester wall units. A slim selection of LPs tilt diagonally on the shelf next to it. As she passes, Peggy slows her steps and crooks her neck to read the spines. No. He isn't there.

'IT'LL TAKE MORE THAN *THAT* TO MAKE MEN DO THE DISHES!'

She catches up with Angie in the kitchen, stood cackling at a painting of a nude woman on a bicycle strategically mounted behind the sink. Peggy, embarrassed, turns instead to the microwave oven. Biding her time, waiting to choose her moment when the moment is chosen for her. On their way out, the glimpse of an acrylic telephone.

Peggy halts in her tracks, wets her lips and clears her throat.

'You do know David still hasn't rung me since Christmas.'

Angie, nodding, lays a sympathetic hand on her arm and 120 decibels of excuse in her ear. Both are all too familiar to Peggy's nervous system.

'I KNOW, SWEETIE! I *KNOW!* BUT YOU MUST UNDERSTAND HE'S BEEN UNDER *A LOT* OF PRESSURE LATELY!'

Always the same. *Work, work, work!* An album he's had to finish, says Angie, and now a lawsuit on his hands against that pig Mr Defries.

'THERE'S LITGATION GOING ON, BUT HE TOLD ME NOT TO WORRY ABOUT IT. NOR SHOULD YOU. I'M NOT GETTING INVOLVED.'

Told *her*, yes, but can't tell his own mother. And from the sounds of it no chance of him coming home anytime soon as he's about to start making some film or other about a spaceman.

'IT'S A VERY BIG THING. HE'S VERY EXCITED ABOUT IT. THE LAST TIME I SPOKE TO HIM HE SOUNDED JUST GREAT!'

BOWIEODYSSEY75

The last time Peggy saw him he didn't. Yesterday evening, on *Top of the Pops*. A four-month-old clip taken from an American TV show, singing his new single, 'Young Americans', just charted at 18 and gridlocked never to climb any higher in a country where the man who plays *Kojak* can literally *talk* his way to number 1. At least David wasn't anywhere near as shocking as on that horrid documentary the other month, and his brown suit *was* very smart. But he still looked a stranger to a square meal and a good night's sleep. It gave Peggy the same old fear.

'I *worry* about him, Angela!' Her voice wobbles. 'He has *no idea* how much I worry! You tell me he's just fine but tomorrow I'll pick up a newspaper and read he's dying in a New York hospital. They wrote that once, you know! I'm his *mother!* I'm a very sensitive person. In fact I'm oversensitive and I get upset *very* easily. I don't even know where he is anymore. You say he's moved to Los Angeles, but *where?* He's my youngest boy, my flesh and blood, and I don't even know *where* he is or what he's doing!'

'OH, NOW! COME HERE . . .'

Peggy is suddenly smothered in warm mink. For the few seconds until Angie releases her it's like being crushed by the Abominable Snowman.

'I *PROMISE* YOU! DAVID *IS* FINE. HE'S ONLY JUST GOT TO LA THIS WEEK. HE NEEDS TO BE THERE BECAUSE OF THE MOVIE. AS SOON AS HE'S SETTLED, HE'LL LET YOU KNOW. *I'LL* LET YOU KNOW!'

'Yes, but where *is* he?'

'STAYING WITH FRIENDS.'

Peggy tuts. 'But *who?*'

'I TOLD YOU . . .'

She and Angie are already 'having' eyes. 'Words' may follow.

'. . . *FRIENDS!*'

THERE'S NO SUCH THING IN LOS ANGELES. Every smile is a lie, every kiss is poison, every lover a Mata Hari, every stranger an enemy you haven't already met. There is no god here except artifice, no virtue except vanity, no vice except kindness, no purpose except personal gain to the detriment of all others. A good day is when you wake up with no knife in your back and a bad one when you go to bed having not stabbed anyone else's. Everyone is either the user or the used, the fooler or the fooled, the greedy or the gobbled, the grabber or the giver, the sucked or the sucker, the blown or the blower, the screwer or the screwed, the Devil or the damned. But nobody is a friend.

David's is a plague carrier, the same as he is, both convinced each other's is the blacker death. This is what binds them. The only way a sick man can feel less so is to look across to the next bed and see someone even sicker. How Glenn sees David and David sees Glenn: a skinny 23-year-old Englishman with bushy hair like Crystal Tipps, an oblong face, a fat jaw, a dimpled chin, eyes a bastard shade of fuck-'em-and-flee-'em brown and a deceptively innocent button nose. The nose that first attracted David's to Glenn's when he crossed his path on tour last year. Love at first snort.

The rest of their bodies have much less in common, aside from the same occupational wears and tears of sex, alcohol and loud amplification. Glenn plays bass and sings in a group who excrete a noxious pong not dissimilar to the Zep, though Deep Purple's isn't so much white bun rock'n'roll as British Rail buffet car: low on taste and curly at the edges. He's just flown off to tour Europe with them, one reason he's offered up his home nestled way up on Tower Grove Drive in the sagebushed slopes of Beverly Hills while he's away. As a refugee on the run from rock'n'roll it has everything David could ever need – privacy, isolation, nearly 3,000 miles of separation from Defries – and the one thing he doesn't. Glenn's housekeeper, Phil, would have to mention in passing that not half a mile away on the other side of Benedict Canyon is the French-style villa where the Manson Family murdered the eight-and-a-half-months-pregnant Sharon Tate before daubing 'PIG' in her blood on the front door. David's new neighbourhood. David's new madhouse.

The house is Glenn's but the madness all his. The same he had in New York, thinking he'd left it there, not noticing it had stowed away in the valise of his chalk-white mind until he hears it whispering to him in the humming dead of night from the pages of his books and the pixels of his TV screen.

Psssst!

Telling him to pick up the telephone receiver and listen for the faint pops and clicks that'll prove he's being monitored by the CIA.

Psssst!

To gather all the sharp knives he can find and stash them under his bed so the Manson Family can't find them.

Psssst!

To raid Glenn's wardrobe for psychically contaminated items of clothing and dump them in the trash.

Psssst!

To write the names of the many witches and warlocks conspiring against him on strips of paper then burn them in the tapering flame of a black candle on the stroke of midnight.

Psssst!

The whispers coming by blinds-drawn day and sleepless night, where there is no such thing as time except that measured in grams and the grinding gaps between. When he is always lonely, but rarely alone.

There are old lovers he can order in like pizza delivery, and new ones plucked from the groping shadows of the Troubadour. There are fellow lepers of the proboscis – burned-out actors and twilight cowpokes of Hollywood and Vine, clinging to him for the same reason he clung to Glenn, racing each other to Hell one tyre-screeching snort after another. There is Adolf Hitler, on his screen, in his books, on repeat behind his eyelids, stoking his envy with the size of his rallies – *Seigy Heildust!* – the century's first stadium rock'n'roll star. There is Thomas Newton trapped on the typewritten page, begging for the kiss of life. There is the Thin White Duke, his cruel leer ever crueller each time David catches himself in the mirror.

And somewhere, far at the bottom of Los Angeles' hostile cesspit of human shambles, having dived too far down in the shit of western civilisation to ever resurface, buried deep in the silt of the as-good-as-dead-if-not-somehow-considerably-worse, there is the exception to the rule. A true friend after all.

He is easily found in a city where nobody walks. The only creature who does. Conspicuous enough without the flashing neon of his platinum hair, the lone strolling shadow in the morning sun baking the billboards of Sunset Strip, the one for *Young Americans* included.

'Jim?'

Unmistakably Iggy.

BOWIEIMAGES75
APICTORIALODYSSEY

Still alive and unwell, still bug-eyed and beautiful, still searching for the Indian rope trick to climb his way back up into rock'n'roll from the bottom of the barrel where the Stooges dumped him. David has no desire to climb there with him, but an Iggy in need is an Iggy indeed, and in two spoonfuls of sugar he finds himself switched-on in the witching hour behind the mixing desk of a claustrophobic four-track studio way up North Cahuenga. The last place David wants to be right now is the last thing Iggy believes he has left. One more chance.

The studio is called Oz but at four in the morning feels more like Kansas. Any wizardry is all David's. The one who comes up with the music, plays every instrument and produces a rough monitor mix. All Jim has to do is walk in the booth and sealclub something Iggyish over the top.

He pulls it out of his head the way a circus clown pulls a loose silk kerchief from their pocket only to keep on tugging a never-ending hankie rope, a spontaneous primal scream of rage and loathing. Through the glass, David watches and listens in biochemical awe. Over three years since they first met, he still can't understand how the world hasn't yet dropped to its knees at Iggy's feet.

'It's the best thing I've ever done.'

Listening to the playback, Iggy seems to agree. One playback being enough. His coat in one hand and tonight's chick in the other, he rises and stumbles towards the door before vanishing into the black hole of the Hollywood night. To score. To shoot. To fuck. To fuck up. To take a Zippo lighter to his Indian rope and watch it burn like a stick of dynamite.

Leaving David alone in the almost dark. Where Iggy has just stood and screamed his soul inside out there is now only emptiness. Just his own thin white reflection staring back from the glass reminding him of all the panics he'd hoped to forget with noise and powder. All of them spelling one name.

Defries.

Then he remembers.

The big showdown. A date has been set and a legal duel agreed in a hotel here in LA where a settlement must be reached one way or the other. Pro David, or pro his monstrous Goliath.

Either side of him the studio speakers buzz in angry electric silence like a low rumbling warning signal. When out of that silence, suddenly, a whisper.

Psssst!

HE IS ALONE, IN THE ALMOST DARK. All those times he passed it in Leicester Square he had no interest in going in. But now, two months later, Patrick slumps low in the flipdown seat of an ABC in Gravesend looking at *The Man with the Golden Gun*. Looking at, but not watching. Staring blankly at the screen but otherwise blind to the cheap kung fu hokum, Britt Ekland's tits and Scaramanga's third nipple. Aware only of light and noise and gunshots and music. And of who he is. And what he's done.

Twice in the last two weeks. Less than two weeks. Only eleven days since he started again, up to his old tricks outside Harrods.

'Madam, can I help you with your shopping?'

Only his odour was too strong — the dowager-repelling bouquet of cheap whisky, bloodlust and the dangling Maltese Cross hidden beneath his shirt. When none of them would surrender their green and gold carrier bags he had no choice but to change tack. Find a quiet square in Belgravia flanked by the white stucco mansions of the very old and very rich. Walk slowly round in circles. And wait.

It was a cinch. She was a slow and shaky 89, fumbling with her house key outside the door to number 13. Unlucky for some. Patrick walked up behind her, jingling his own keys as if he lived in the same block. That's what she assumed and let him in behind her.

Halfway up the stairs he pulled the old 'Missus, I'm feeling faint' routine. She took pity and invited him as far as the threshold of her hallway to wait while she fetched him a glass of water. Then he followed her inside and clamped his hands around her neck. Big hands with slender fingers, digging into her throat, squeezing and squeezing until her face went blue, her lips black and her body limp.

'Bye, bye, baby . . .'

That bloody song. You couldn't move for it that week. You still can't. Always on the radio, like the ones he stole from her flat, two little transistors, after he spent the rest of the afternoon there, her corpse in one room, him in another watching her telly in her favourite armchair until he dozed off. Had he slept any longer he could have been caught red-handed. On his way out he passed his victim's granddaughter coming up the stairs. She didn't even notice him.

'Bye, bye, baby . . .'

That should have been the end of it. As he made his mind up, the end of him. After the next two days in a malted haze, around midnight last Wednesday he climbed down off the platform at Stockwell underground station and stumbled into the lightless mouth of hell. If a train didn't kill him head on, then the electric rails would. Or would have were he not spotted by staff who switched off the current. He staggered blind drunk through the northbound tunnel to Oval where the coppers were waiting for him. Arrested and questioned, he spent the next six days under observation in a local psychiatric ward. Again he attempted suicide, this time with his pyjama cord, and again he failed. So did the hospital. Though they diagnosed him as 'probably of psychopathic personality' the doctors lacked 'sufficient grounds' to detain him any further. They kicked him back out on the streets this Tuesday.

'Bye, bye, baby . . .'

Wednesday, he was snatching handbags in Chelsea again. Thursday, quelling the beast with more alcohol. So reeking with scotch that when he finally made it home to the Cowdreys in Grantham Road it sparked a family argument whether to let him stay or not. Their eldest son told him to go. If he wanted a bed for the night he should knock on his old pal, Father Crean, the priest in Kent who he stole money off two years ago but, begging the forgiveness of the Lord, refused to press charges.

'Go and see your old queer vicar!'

The words hit Patrick like dumdum bullets. The Cowdreys stood back while he seized a broom handle and started smacking the floor, screaming how he was going to 'bash that priest till he's got no head!' If only to shut him up, they relented, letting him stay. He passed out on their settee fully clothed.

Where he woke up today. Friday. Leaving abruptly before breakfast, taking the Tube to Waterloo station where he bought a return ticket to Gravesend where his estranged mother lives. Just a two-mile walk from the village of that 'old queer vicar'.

He didn't die easily. He had fight in him. Not a strong man, but strong in the belief that God would somehow save him. Which he didn't.

It was teatime when Father Crean came home to his cottage opposite St Catherine's Convent and found Patrick waiting. He guessed immediately, seeing it in Patrick's eyes the way they all saw it in his eyes. The terror of knowing they'd be the last eyes they'd ever look into.

The priest tried to barricade himself in the bathroom. Patrick battered the door in, forcing him struggling into the tub, holding him down as he slashed at his neck and face with a knife until the blade bent. Then he swapped it for an axe. It split the skull easy as chopping wood. One loud wet crunch. After that, the priest stopped thrashing. The more the blood spouted the more it excited Patrick, hacking and hacking until he could see the exposed grey jelly of the brain. Father Crean, not quite dead, feebly raised his fingers to touch it as he slid down further into the tub.

He'd done what he'd promised. Bashed that priest till he'd got no head. It was still on his shoulders but you couldn't call it a head anymore. Just a neck with a hot dribbling wound on top; a sticky red ball of torn flesh and pulverised bone with not enough features left to make even half a face.

Sat on the rim, Patrick put the plug in and ran the taps, watching the body slowly submerge, the water reddening around it. When almost full he turned them off and left it there. Bobbing in blood soup.

'Bye, bye, baby . . .'

The strange thing is, there's not a spot of it on him. His last look at the bathroom was like shutting the door on a slaughterhouse but to see him now you'd think he'd been sat here in the pictures all day. Alone, in the almost dark. Staring blankly at the screen. Aware only of light and noise and gunshots and music. And of who he is.

Ja, ja! Franklin Bollvolt the First! A name to be feared and remembered like Hitler's!

And what he's done.

EIGHT

GOOD EEEEVENING! This is Don Travanti broadcasting to you LIVE from the heart of Los Angeles for what promises to be a thrilling evening in the ring here at the Plaza in Century City. Joining me in the commentary box tonight is Howard Weitz.

Good evening and thank you, Don. Yes, thrilling, you might say, in fact some have already been calling this one THE fight of the century.

Certainly the most important fight in either career and I'm sure everyone watching at home who's been following the headlines will know why. This is a huge bout for a huge belt and no love lost between these contenders.

Oh, it's a grudge match, Don, no two ways about. A very tough one to call.

Tough's the word. I don't think we've seen a management and artist showdown like it and I think we're in for a big punching fight tonight. Tell me, Howie, you've been visiting the workouts at both camps all week, you've seen their form. What's your estimation of what sort of fight we're in for?

I'd say both contenders are looking in great shape. One of the big tests today is how quickly Bowie gets warmed up and whether Defries will fight around him for

BOWIEODYSSEY**75**

a little bit or really go at it. Obviously, there've been a lot of health rumours in the Bowie camp.

And from what you saw, how is he?

Undoubtedly, he's the bonier, shall we say, but he's a got very strong corner in his lawyer, Lippman. So I think we might be surprised at how fierce a challenge Bowie can bring tonight.

And what about Defries?

He can be a slow starter, as we know, so there may be some vulnerability in the early rounds depending on how he plays it. So far he's been the quieter of the two in the lead up. Most of those headlines you mentioned have all been generated by the Bowie camp.

Maybe just refresh us on some of those for the sake of anyone who's not been paying such close attention?

Sure thing, Don. Well, the gist of it is 'BOWIE SUES MANAGER'.

It's a contract thing, right?

Right. Bowie wants out, and this showdown has been on the cards for many months now, going back to last fall, maybe even earlier. He's been very unhappy with how Defries has been managing his finances in terms of his percentage, in terms of how he's been using the profits from Bowie's earnings to plough into other Mainman projects.

Mainman being Defries's company.

That's correct. Basically tonight is the crunch because a settlement has to be reached one way or the other. So I really do think we're looking at a knockout situation. Either Bowie finishes Defries early or Defries takes Bowie all the way to the cleaners. This one won't be won on points as nobody wants a draw. Somebody's going down and staying down for the eight count.

SIMONGODDARD

Who's your money on, Howie?

Oh, I really can't call it. I don't think we should underestimate either man. Bowie has the talent and the muscle in his corner, but we all know about Defries when it comes to legal uppercuts. It's a case of power versus technique. I think this one's going to be an epic battle and I wouldn't be at all surprised if it ends up a very close fight.

We should probably also mention tonight's referee, Laurence Myers. A very interesting choice.

He is. As some viewers may know, Myers has history with both. Five years ago he took Defries under his wing as his business partner, during which time he also helped build Bowie's career.

Then Defries bought Myers out.

He did – that was just after Ziggy back in '72. So he's got no personal stake in this, but he knows how both boys operate. He's been flown over from England to act as mediator and was instrumental in the choice of venue here at the Plaza. Actually, that's been the hardest part: finding a neutral territory both sides would agree on. If I know Myers, he'll want a good clean fight.

Well, we're about to find out just how clean as there's commotion in the corridor and I think – yes? – they're heading to the ring right now. Is it? Yes, it's Defries!

It's Defries, and, boy, there's a face of determination!

Very cool, very calm, and of course it wouldn't be Defries, would it, if he wasn't tugging on his trademark Cuban cigar?

No, it would not, and that baby sure is a monster!

Shaking hands now with referee Myers and the RCA team before Defries takes his place on the sofa at one end of the suite and . . . oh, now there's

BOWIEODYSSEY75

more movement at the door, and we don't see him yet but we assume from the roar . . . now here's Bowie!

David Bowie, making his way through, just visible behind his lawyers, smartly dressed in a dark suit, wearing dark glasses.

Those won't be coming off, will they, Howie?

I very much doubt it. And here he is, stepping into the centre of the ring. He's looking very thin, but very serious and his nose is twitching. I'd say that's a sure sign he means business. And – wow! – the excitement begins to mount . . . Just drink this in for a second, folks, already an incredible sight. Here's Bowie and Defries finally together under the same roof after months of rancour.

Incredible, Howie, but, yep, here they are, and just look at the body language. Defries isn't even flinching. Not a muscle. And no reaction from Bowie either as he takes his place on the opposite sofa. The poker faces are ON!

Well, Don, we'll soon see whose drops first. So now Myers is addressing both fighters, laying down the rules of the game. No holding, break when he says break.

If we listen in, he's actually appealing for an early settlement.

I don't think there's much hope of that.

I entirely agree. These men want blood, but Myers is arguing his best.

We have to remember Myers has profited nicely out of his past associations with both men. His take seems to be that if they can't find a truce the only real winners here will be their respective lawyers.

The problem is: do either of them trust Myers? You can cut the suspicion in the air with a knife.

Could be. Like you say, both Bowie and Defries might think Myers is secretly working for the other side.

Well, whatever he's said it hasn't worked because the briefcases are open and there goes the bell and we are ready to go! Round number one!

And it's a packed house here in the Century City Plaza as Bowie opens up fast, his lawyer Lippman urging him to jab Defries.

Jabbing but not connecting. Defries is not an easy target. He's bobbing and weaving, shifting left to right. Bowie doesn't seem to be able to catch him, but he's still jabbing with a light glancing blow over the shoulder.

That's another good left! And, look, it's not just Lippman, Bowie's got the whole firm of Cooper, Epstein, Hurewitz & Mark, as well as Balin and Company. A good combination of punches there. Bowie looking very clear-eyed.

And there goes another hard left, and Defries shakes his head. I don't know if it's because of his reach, but Bowie doesn't seem to be throwing everything into his punches but . . . *OH!* Now that was a great flurry there as Bowie vies for damages for breach of contract!

This is more than a declaration of termination we're seeing here! Bowie is getting on the inside, taunting Mainman to produce an account of all funds involving him over the past five years! And suddenly Defries looks more unsure in this opening round than we thought.

Or does he? Look at him smiling as he takes those jabs – and that cigar still hasn't left his mouth! And here's Bowie already lighting his second cigarette with less than a minute to go in round one.

I still don't think Defries is making enough use of the ring. This is not the Defries we are used to seeing, Don. He looks in danger of getting tied up on the ropes if he's not careful. Just fifteen seconds to go and unless he can pull something out fast I'd say this round is definitely all Bowie's.

He's not giving Defries any chance to move around and fight his own fight, and now it's three, two, one, and there's the bell! A great round for Bowie!

BOWIEODYSSEY75

As exciting a first round as we've seen in Century City! They're looking very confident over in the Bowie corner. I suppose the big story in this game is whether he can continue like that.

Over in the Defries corner, though, no real damage done either. That cigar has barely gone down a quarter-inch!

I think you may be right, Don. That was a good start from Bowie, but he needs to get cleaner shots if he wants to take him out. Only one round in, this fight is anything but over.

Just waiting now for the signal from referee Myers. There it goes, and it's round two, and Defries is already out quicker than the last round and he's not shying away from Bowie and – *OH!* – now that was a good right glove and I think Bowie looks a little bit hurt by that punch.

A bruising exchange from Defries as he maintains full financial rights of fifty per cent on EVERYTHING Bowie has recorded up until now!

Bowie's looking anxiously over at his corner, but Lippman doesn't have any reply and nor does he, and now Defries is on the attack again, another good one-two, and he's scoring heavily with that big reach of his. Now looking to work the body.

And this is a complete reversal from the last round with Bowie taking a good battering as Defries reminds him that his contract doesn't expire until – that is one wicked left hook to the body! – September 1982! That's another seven and a half years!

Now that must have hurt. Defries continues to build up a sweat and work downstairs, and suddenly Bowie throws a wild left hand. He's starting to look whipped, but he's still on his feet even though he's been hit with solid lefts that would have felled an ordinary man. What an astounding second round!

It's been a dandy!

The Bowie camp are watching the clock, desperate for that bell. They need him back in the corner to patch him up and refocus and, right on cue, there it goes for the end of round two.

An extraordinary round! We knew Defries was maybe being a bit cautious in the first, but that was magnificent. And, I really don't know, Don, at this point I would say Defries is looking like he's starting to have the edge. Look at Bowie. He already seems tired, and I think we can even see some swelling around the eyes. Lippman is in his ear, and it's a very different mood in the Bowie corner from the end of the first round.

Defries seems positively raging to get back out, and here's referee Myers returning to the centre of the ring and here we go again – round three!

And Defries is out quickly and opening up fast. Bowie still looks shaken from the seven-year punch in round two. He's gamely trying to fight back, but I fear he might already be spent, and Defries just keeps on with the lefts, toe to toe, and he's pushing Bowie back up against the ropes. Left and right and – WOAH! – that first punch did no damage but the second one did.

This is a worrying time for Bowie's corner because Defries is dealing up plenty of punishment, not wasting his punches! Telling Bowie he'll be taking 16 per cent of Bowie's gross earnings from all sources!

Defries is the aggressor now, and Bowie's corner are yelling at him to back off and keep moving, but he's got him in a jam and – WOW! He's taking him for a slice of all future fees, royalties, rents, bonuses, gifts, profits, proceeds, allowances, shares of stock and stock options!

And Bowie's having an awful lot of trouble coping with Defries's fast hands! It's one blow after another now! This is going to be Bowie's cost of cutting free, having Defries skim him for all future work in television, motion pictures, radio, night clubs, vaudeville, theatres and presentation houses! Defries is going all out now! Legitimate theatre productions, musical shows of any kind including but not limited to Broadway and Off Broadway musicals! Recordings of any kind by any means or methods whether now known or hereafter to become known! Hotels, resorts, fairs, concerts and one-nighters! The pace is tremendous!

He's really got Bowie nailed and he isn't finished yet! He's going for commercial endorsements where Bowie's name, likeness or performances are utilised! Songwriting, whether as a composer or lyricist, and whether alone or in collaboration with others . . . Bowie looking increasingly helpless . . . still more – musical arranging, conducting and directing as a producer of any recordings of any kind by any means or methods whether now known or hereafter to become known . . . Bowie's legs are looking rubbery and he's flailing away, the speed of Defries simply outclassing him and he's still not finished! He wants him for the sale, lease, license or other disposition of literary, dramatic, musical productions, radio and/or television production shows, whether live, filmed, recorded, syndicated or in any other form! Don, this is a slaughtering!

Myers is looking over to the Bowie corner. Still a full minute left in this round – are they going to let him take any more? Lippman looks like he doesn't know what to do!

Bowie is bleeding heavily now, I think they might have to end this because here's Defries really opening up with those combinations! And Bowie's staggering! He looks badly hurt and ANOTHER solid left and . . . it's PERPETUITY! Right on the button! Right on the jaw! Defries has got Bowie owing in perpetuity! And surely this has to be the end and . . . HE'S DOWN! BOWIE'S DOWN! MYERS STARTS THE COUNT AND NOW THERE GOES THE TOWEL! BOWIE'S CORNER THROWS IN THE TOWEL, AND IT'S ALL OVER! DEFRIES HAS WON! OH, MY! WON EASILY! BOWIE IS DEFEATED! DEFRIES IS VICTORIOUS!

THERE IT IS! IT'S ALL OVER! Well – *phewie!* – I'm not sure that was quite *the* fight of the century, but we've never seen anything like it, have we? Just LOOK at the difference between the two corners! Bowie is a broken man, while Defries has another dozen writs in him easy. Howie, how on earth would you sum up what we've just witnessed here tonight?

I tell ya, Defries has pulled off a miracle! Let's just recap some of those killer punches, Don. He's walked away with everything he had before he walked in the ring plus a sizeable cut of Bowie's income for the rest of his life!

Everything he had before he walked in, apart from Bowie's management. If it's any consolation, Bowie is now free, isn't he, Howie?

He is, but what price freedom, Don? What price?

And is there any poetic justice in this at all? If we go back five years to when Bowie fought against his previous manager, Ken Pitt? Pitt was the sore loser that time.

He was, but I wouldn't call this one justice. What we saw tonight was a straightforward demolition job. Defries has demolished Bowie and his legal team, and to some extent RCA. There's only one winner tonight, and it's the man with the cigar.

Well, from this man without a cigar, all that remains is for me to thank you all at home for joining us for this unforgettable fight night live from the heart of Los Angeles. Until next week, it's goodbye from me, Don Travanti, my colleague Howie Weitz and the whole team here at Century City Plaza. Thank you, and goodnight!

NINE

IT'S TOO LATE when David asks for a mezuzah – a small parchment of Hebrew verses from the Torah rolled up inside a thin case roughly the size of a finger of Fudge – and nails it to the doorpost of his bedroom. The same goes for the cross he starts wearing, a simple gold crucifix on a gold chain given to him by his late father. Not fussy whose God protects him now, the critical hour for divine intervention has come and gone. The nightmare has happened. His monster has won.

The bedroom isn't his own but nor is it Glenn's. The phantom rustles of the Manson Family's creepy-crawling have scared him out of Benedict Canyon into the slopes of West Hollywood to lick his wounds with Lippman and his wife, Nancy, in their Spanish bungalow amongst the jacarandas and magnolias wiggling up Kings Road, north of Sunset Strip. The house of the defeated.

In the aftermath of their massacre in Century City, Lippman scrambles in the wreckage for any tin drum to bang some hollow victory.

'You're free now,' he consoles David. 'Free from Defries, free from Mainman. That's the most important thing.'

Like being told your whole family's been killed in a car crash but the most important thing is the vehicle's now yours to drive: smashed windscreen, dented fenders, twisted axle and all. Free in soul but not in salary. Held at ransom for the remainder of his life. Whatever he does,

SIMONGODDARD

whatever songs he records, whatever concerts he plays, whatever films he makes, the choices are all his but the pay packet will always be the same. Gross minus taxes plus the pound of flesh to Tony Defries.

'*In perpetuity.*'

Everything and anything David does from now on, the breath from his lungs, the notes plucked from his fingers, the sweat off his back, will keep dropping dimes in Defries's piggy bank like pennies from heaven. However rich he gets, he'll never be as rich as he should be, and however poor, he'll always be that extra bit poorer. David's body is no longer his own but another man's walking investment portfolio, at least sixteen per cent of it in permanent hock. Roughly the surface area of his skin. From his face to his cock, the sack of his balls and the cheeks of his arse. All of it the equivalent intellectual property of a Co-op's own brand Colonel Parker with liquid assets for blood and an adding machine where his ticker should be.

'*In perpetuity.*'

Forever and ever, amen.

It's always the most desperate who finally find God when they've nothing else left to believe in. David isn't taking any chances. He's recruiting deities like *The Magnificent Seven*: Yahweh, Jesus, Ein Sof, Nuit, the Sun, faithful to none but smash-and-grabbing all for his deranged Gnosticism, making up his own prayers, rituals and a new sacred language out of his doodled runish Latin script he names the 'Isolaric Alphebeth'.

Seeing one crucifix around David's neck, Lippman buys him another larger one, the kind Rasputin might have dangled outside his tunic. He takes to wearing both like an Oxford Street suitcase evangelist. Religion is a new drug, constantly fed by the old one and just as addictive if an in-no-way-close second in his hierarchy of bodily needs. When it comes to apostolic devotion, David still knows which side his daily bread is buttered.

It is not just that he is vulnerable. It is much worse: he is bored. The Devil merely finds work for idle hands whereas God sentences them to indefinite hard labour. David is shipwrecked in Los Angeles with nothing to do and nowhere to go other than out of his mind at increasing velocity. He still has a script to learn and a role to prepare, but production of *The Man Who Fell to Earth* has been delayed while Mr Roeg continues to haggle for studio finances. With *Young Americans* in the lower reaches of this week's American Top 10, there's nothing stopping him booking a local studio to start making the follow-up. But freshly straitjacketed by the knowledge he'd still be treadmilling for Defries, he hasn't the will. He could carry on making demos with Iggy, only Iggy has since disappeared, the latest mentholated mumbles from the snitches on skid row that he's testing the diagnostic mettle of UCLA's Neuropsychiatric Hospital. Where David should possibly consider joining him, were he himself not so close to the cell he can see the padding.

In absence of studio time, tour or shooting schedule, madness becomes a form of gainful self-employment. Hungry for overtime, he rallies fresh artillery to his war against sleep to maintain maximum productivity. To the casual observer, much of it just within the furthest margins of sane behaviour. Abstract paintings and weird drawings based around pentagrams and the Kabbalah Tree of Life. More written fragments to cut up and add to the plotless narrative of *The Return of the Thin White Duke*. Sculptures made from found objects including a toy baby doll, a globe and a penis comprising a foreskin of rolled-up 3-D postcards with a Mickey Mouse pencil sharpener for the glans. Seemingly harmless creative mania.

But if that were the case, the day wouldn't dawn when Nancy Lippman rises, stretches and ambles to her kitchen to prepare breakfast for herself and her husband, opening the door of her fridge to find beside the milk and the orange juice a rogue bottle containing a clear off-colour liquid she doesn't immediately recognise. Only when she picks it up and sniffs it.

Were she a biological chemist, under laboratory conditions she'd be able to verify it as the fluid generated in the kidneys of an adult Homo sapiens whose diet is chiefly tropane alkaloids supplemented by occasional lactose and traces of capsicum. As it is, Nancy's all too well acquainted with her lodger's paintings, penis sculptures and rambling late–night conversations about the witches he's seen lurking in the shrubbery and the magic magnetism of bodily fluids.

That bottle in her fridge, she knows without having to ask, is the chilled piss of David Bowie.

★

SIMONGODDARD

LIKE HOLY WATER back in the country he calls home where his followers pine for his return like the Second Coming. The bottled urine of our lord David Bowie. Ascended to an unreachable heaven beyond their grasp, their only comfort the wild prophecies of cheap newsprint that he might yet perform miracles on a British stage this summer. All they have is iconography. Posters, T-shirts, badges, magazines and his new album, *Young Americans*. A different David to any they've worshipped before, stripped of any fancy dress and space opera – a Saturday Night Bowie for the over 21s, no jeans allowed and ladies get in free before 11 – yet a test of their faith they pass in enough numbers to take all the way to number 2. The reason it can't reach number 1 is because number 1 is now a graveyard of antiquity, where the best of Engelbert Humperdinck has just spent three weeks at the top, and where David hasn't a mission against the equally insurmountable *20 Greatest Hits* of Tom Jones. At 33⅓ the future has died. The past has come and come to stay. The only songs are yesterday's.

'Bye, bye, baby . . .'

Still the number 1 single: a song first recorded 11 years ago by the Four Seasons about an adulterer telling his fancy piece he must sadly give her the heave-ho and crawl back to the wife; sung by four unwed Scotsmen aged 18 to 26, forbidden to cultivate personal relationships by their paedophile manager; selling by the hundreds of thousands to schoolgirls led to believe their tartan idols are chaste, teetotal milk drinkers, one of whom – preferably Les or Woody, ideally not Derek – will one day lift their tulle veil and kiss them at the altar to the envy of every other virgin in Christendom. It's been at the top for four weeks and will stay there another two before being elbowed off by 'Oh, Boy!', a song first recorded 18 years ago by Buddy Holly and the Crickets about how wowzah it feels being in love, sung by a quartet of geezers from Surrey just four pairs of tights away from playing armed robbers in the next episode of *The Sweeney*. Pocket money for old rope.

At 45, the revolution is over. There is the old glam of Sweet, the sham-glam of Kenny, the cheeky soul of Jim Gilstrap and Moments and Whatnauts, the schmaltz of 'Love Me Love My Dog' and the musical party tickler of 'Funky Gibbon' by the Goodies, who only two weeks ago killed a 50-year-old Scotsman who died laughing at their sketch of an

'Ecky Thump' duel between a black pudding and a set of bagpipes. His widow wrote them a thank-you letter.

The kids crying for change blow their pimply noses in vain. Brit rock '75 is, at best, the Zep out-Wondering Stevie with 'Trampled Underfoot' and the Syrian air strike of 'Kashmir'. At worst, Rick Wakeman's *The Myths And Legends Of King Arthur And The Knights Of The Round Table*. Music for young men who don't even like music but need something to listen to between wanking over old posters of Sonja Kristina and rereading *Lord of the Rings*.

Far out on the non-charting fringes, the supposed rebirth of rock'n'roll as forecast last year in the sweatbox function rooms of London publand dies during labour. On stage, Dr Feelgood are a coiled spring: on record, slack elastic. It breaks the *NME*'s heart to report their debut album is *'not that hot'* but it isn't. The Feelgoods can pack out the Village Blues Club in Dagenham eight days a week but in the Top 10 *Tubular Bells* chimes on regardless. Someday, maybe a *real* uprising will emerge − a group of heroic young rascals angry enough to crash the Zeppelin, say no to Yes, void the Floyd and put Wakeman to sleep. Someday.

In shorter hair and speedier rhythm, the one new cult is a separatist religion founded in the North, and even their hymns are all old, just unfamiliar. Their churches are sprung-floorboarded casinos and Mecca ballrooms, their Eucharist amphetamines, their vestments the baggiest of Oxford bags, their prayers recited in sweat, their glossolalia not spoken in tongues but spine-breaking acrobatics. They preach community through exclusivity, piety through obscurity, but these are worrying times for the precious priests of northern soul. Its gospel has spread further than they'd like, to the sports-vested epilepsy of Wigan's Chosen Few on *Top of the Pops* and weekly charts in *Record Mirror*. Some of their most sacred psalms − the unfettering thrills of Dean Parrish's 'I'm On My Way' and Frankie Valli's 'The Night' − have even been blasphemed by the scourge of mass popularity and hijacked by the Top 40. No man is an island, but northern soul would prefer to remain the St Kilda of Seventies youth culture; alone and backflipping to the one copy of a rare Motown test pressing no other human has ever heard and, if they've any say in the matter, never will.

This, the school-gravy-brown England of *Young Americans*, twisting in ever decreasing bygone circles like a lithograph by M. C. Escher. On

SIMONGODDARD

TV, Dixon is still bobbying the beat of Dock Green, Ena Sharples is still bending the ear of Minnie Caldwell and Doctor Who is still fighting the Daleks. For those with black-and-white sets it might as well be 1965.

It is an unticking time of hits but no anthems, pin-ups but no heroes, stars but no starmen. Apart from one.

His name is Sky. A young alien with blond hair and strange eyes, 'part angel, part waif', sent by his race of homo-superiors to sort things out on Earth after a future catastrophe known as 'The Chaos'. Except a freak dimensional timeslip throws him off course, stranding him in the pre-Chaos teenage England of 1975. Airing Monday teatimes on ITV straight after *Clapperboard*.

'He seems to be getting quite a following,' says *Sky*'s producer. 'You can imagine what sort of confusion it would cause if a lad popped up and said he was from outer space and had come to put right all the thing's we'd been doing wrong.'

The boy who fell to Earth. No, we don't have to imagine. And as the country spins backwards regardless of record speed, we can only yearn.

Oh, David. Where *are* you?

SOMEWHERE IN LOS ANGELES. That's as much as Angie knows.

'DAVID? *WHERE* ARE YOU?'

On the end of a telephone, but whose telephone, in whose house, in which part of the city, he won't say.

'WITCHES? D . . . DAV. . . STOP! *WHAT* ARE YOU TALKING ABOUT?'

The witches of Los Angeles. Two in particular who are determined to steal his magnetism for their own demonic purposes. Everything he's been reading about in his well-thumbed copy of *Psychic Self-Defense*. The etheric energy in his hair-combings, nail-clippings, dead skin, shit, piss and spunk, any of which can be used to curse him along with cast-off clothes, bed linen and anything else he's sat on, lain in or touched for any great length of time.

So far, he's outfoxed the witches by hiding his urine, but his semen is much less secure. See, these witches – as he tries to explain to his wife, long-distance, in dot-dashing disconnected sentences punctuated by neckripping sniffs – are sex witches, trapping him with their irresistible bodies so that he'll have no choice but to inseminate them. Once he deposits his seed in their fertile witchy wombs they intend to carry his bastard child up until the point of birth. Then, as he tells Angie, they'll offer up the squealing newborn as a blood sacrifice to The Evil One.

'*DAVID?*'

She stands at her living-room window, receiver in one hand looking out at the rain-brewing clouds of an April morning and the motionless Chelsea street below. Grey mundanity in her eyeballs. Technicolor lunacy in her eardrums.

'*WHO* WON'T LET YOU GO?'

Behind her, Zowie plays with his nanny, Marion, while Marcus the dog flops in the corner, sheepish brown eyes wondering how long it will take before anyone notices he's broken wind again. Registering the alarm in Angie's voice, Marion prudently takes Zowie's hand and tiptoes him out of the room. Eager to flee the scene of the crime, Marcus bolts upright and lollops after them.

'WA . . . WAIT! THERE'S A *WARLOCK* AS WELL AS THE WITCHES?'

Angie knows David's voice well enough to know she's definitely talking to her husband of five years. But beyond the familiarity of tone and accent she may as well be on the line to a complete stranger. Some prank caller babbling about witchcraft and Devil babies, suckering her in to join him incanting 'salagadoola menchika boola' before slapping his thigh with 'Smile! You're on *Candid Camera*!' If only it were that funny.

'JUST GET OUT OF THERE NOW! WALK OUT AND HAIL A CAB!'

Angie knows it isn't. Not remotely. Her David is a man of a thousand moods and she has a mental index card for them all. This is a new one – to file under T for 'They're Coming To Take Me Away, Ha-Haaa!'

Her suitcase is open as soon as she's off the phone. He doesn't ask her to come. It's just the unwritten vow of their marriage.

'*I, Angie, take you, David, to be my lawful wedded husband so that every time you fuck up I'll drop everything in my life and jump on the next ten-hour Transatlantic flight according to God's holy law.*'

When she thinks of all those starfucking fools who think they're close to him – the so-called friends, the company sycophants, the lovers, the pushers – but when the shit hits the fan there's not one of them with the stomach to bend down and scoop it up with their bare hands.

Just her.

The same indispensable Wonder Woman who's been scooping it up for the last five years. And here she is again. About to fly halfway round the world to wade waist deep in yet more David shit.

It's only when she picks the phone up again to ring the airport she finally smells the dog fart.

AFTER A WEEK OF CONFINEMENT shitting in a bucket he gets used to the smell. He gets used to all of it. The hard whiteness of the brick walls like cricket bats to the slightest sound. The barred and meshed postage stamp of daylight high up in the wall above his grey metal bed. The blinking shadows behind the spyhole checking to see he hasn't hung himself. The percussive slam and jingle of cell doors and keys like the constant drips of water torture. The daytime echoes of shouts and jeers. The nighttime ones of the finally snapped and screaming. The regimented wake up, slop out and lights out. The taste of the metal tray still clinging to every unnourishing forkful he brings back to his cell. The behind-hand whispers and suspicious eyes in the exercise yard. The feeling of not being anywhere on earth, even though he knows he must only be a mile at most from the Bowie-birthing streets he used to call home. HMP Brixton. Here three weeks and Patrick is already an old lag.

They picked him up two days after he killed the priest. The dots were easily joined.

The police were called after one of the nuns discovered Father Crean where Patrick had left him, brained and marinading in bloody water. The DI in Gravesend station remembered Crean's name from two years earlier. Hard to forget, when a priest is robbed but doesn't want the culprit to be prosecuted. Patrick's name was there in the case notes. A stab in the dark but the only lead they had. They spent the next day chasing his records back to London where the *Evening News* stuck its own knife in Saturday night with the front-page headline 'MURDER HUNT

BOWIEODYSSEY75

AS NUNS FIND DEAD PRIEST'. That hunt ending Sunday morning when they tracked him to the Cowdreys in Stockwell. He didn't resist arrest.

At first they charged him with one murder. Now it's three. His fingerprints grassed him up for last year's killing of the widow in Chelsea and the other last month in Belgravia. Those he confessed to, but it could be worse. There's seven more they can't pin on him. The spinster he battered to death in Kentish Town. Others in Hackney and Westcliffe-on-Sea. A tobacconist in Finsbury Park. A woman and her five-year-old grandson in Hadley Green. And a tramp who drowned after Patrick punted him off Hungerford Bridge.

'Bye, bye, baby . . .'

Still number 1, the faint trebly buzz from a transistor radio down the other end of F Wing.

No date has yet been set for his trial at the Old Bailey. Until it is, all he can do is sit, reflect, write in his prison journal or lie staring up at his bare cell walls. Then close his eyes and pretend he's back in his room in the Cowdreys', saluting in dreams of Franklin Bollvolt. Beneath his favourite picture of Hitler.

TEN

HE'S NO WORSE than Angie expected and no better than she feared. A sick stray animal some too-good Samaritan might scrape off the roadside before rushing to the vet in a cardboard box. Skinny, shaky and in dire want of nutrition. His head couldn't look any thinner if it was vacuum packed. Like a portrait by Egon Schiele: finely-drawn, long in the face and just the minimum splodge of colour upon the cheekbones suggestive of pulsing life. Yet David somehow elevates emaciation to heights of male elegance not seen in an Englishman since they stopped rationing.

Her first task is to find him a home of his own and stop leaning on the Lippmans. If only for the sake of their fridge, they're not as sorry to see him go as they make out. But houses in Hollywood are like other planets in the solar system – they all have their own weird atmosphere. It's near impossible to find some place where some famous actor or actress hasn't lived, loved, been murdered or committed violent suicide bequeathing the property to a hostile ghost. Add the passing of time and these same landmark legends tend to run riot like an unpruned privet, blessing or cursing every neighbouring house with the same infamy fifty doors in either direction.

Or as many as 245. Marilyn Monroe lived briefly at 882 Doheny Drive. David moves into number 637 but what's a fifth of a mile between celebrity drug addicts. *Mi casa es su casa*. Boop-boop-a-doop.

It wasn't Angie's first choice, just the first that passed David's paranormal specifications as the odds-on most witch-proof. A comparatively modest one-storey house built in the mid-Forties by a brutalist architect whose overzealous value of privacy extended to the omission of all but a few concessionary windows and the central feature of an indoor swimming pool. From the main road it could easily be mistaken for some sort of private crematorium, the tall chimney at its north end somehow naked without a billowing plume of black smoke raining coffin ash over the street palms. For all the life David brings, it might as well be.

That Angie never once opens either of its fridges to be confronted with her husband's freshly passed water offers the fleeting false hope the change of scene has placed his first foot upon the road to recovery. Very fleeting.

David had initially warmed to the house because of its interior Egyptian décor. Hollywood by numbers, where the film sets extend far beyond the backlot filling even the tiniest lounges and bedrooms with decorative tributes to Cecil B. DeMille. But one night in the master bedroom and he wakes up shivering with the same old Mummy's curse.

Nothing changes. The evils. The fears. The bodies falling out of the sky and the sudden movements in the bushes. The sheets of paper stuck to the walls so he can draw giant pentagrams, Kabbalah symbols or his own Isolaric Alphebeth. The crank interpretations of obscure Edwardian books on the Tarot and ceremonial magic. The conviction a coven of witches has yet to surrender its vow to steal his soul for the Antichrist. The increasing fascination with the magnetism of Hitler, the manipulation of Goebbels and the symbolism of the swastika. The thin white dreams of becoming a fascist dictator. The psychedelic nightmare reality that comes with not having slept for five days straight. The $200 daily avalanche of shit wadding up his nostrils keeping him awake. The hysterics whenever Angie suggests he should maybe wad a little less. The carton after carton of milk and the monotonous ritualistic slicing of peppers into the slimmest of chewable strips. Nothing. Just the absence of piss in the fridge.

Apart from his one new hobby. He discovered it the other week when he finally tracked down Iggy to his neuropsychiatric ward in UCLA Hospital. Tradition decreed visitors should bring their sick friends bunches of grapes, but David reckoned his old pal Jim would prefer a bag of blow and reckoned rightly; when it came time to leave, it wasn't nearly so easy for the nurses to tell which one of them ought best be let back out on the street as when David arrived.

The hobby was waiting for him in a doctor's office in the same wing. As Thelma Schnee she once wrote screenplays for Fifties B pictures about human brains transplanted into rampaging cyborgs. As Thelma Moss she gave it up to pursue something less scientific, now an expert in the field of parapsychology. Telekinesis, astral projection, electronic voice phenomenon. All that Rod Serling wavy gravy anyone can entertain if they've an open mind or a slagheap of coke where their logic should be.

Dr Moss's particular area of expertise is a form of electromagnetic photography pioneered in Soviet Russia by a man named Kirlian. It involves a special machine that looks a bit like an oscilloscope crossed with an oven hob but operates more along the lines of an electric chair, using high voltage to capture the coronal discharge of stationary objects upon a photographic plate – mystic energies and psychic auras unseen with the naked eye. The machines themselves are costly and rare, to be used under strict supervision. The last thing anyone harbouring any sense of medical professionalism would allow is to lend one to a cerebrally unhinged rock star who won't cut his toenails for fear they'll be swept up and sprinkled into the same bubbling cauldron as eye of newt and wool of bat. But then Dr Moss is 57: David, a waxily handsome 28.

Back in Doheny Drive, David plugs it in and the West Hollywood grid skips a heartbeat. He takes his father's crucifix off the chain around his neck and places it on the hotplate. Beneath it, he presses the tip of his forefinger. A flick of the switch and enough current to flash-fry a dormouse slowly pulses through his metacarpal. He sits, skeleton buzzing, and waits for the exposure: a faint outline of the cross and a thin black ring where his finger touched. Half an hour later he repeats the experiment after another gram has taken the northbound express to his olfactory nerves. This time the cross radiates with divine white heat and he can barely see his fingertip for the mass coronal ejection exploding around it.

A sign.

As he always suspected, lacking any evidence, but now here's all the proof he needs. Clear as a burning bush.

To think Angie keeps telling him to wad a little *less*? Well, here's the word of the Lord and it couldn't be any plainer if a heaped spoonful reached down from out of the sky and shoved itself under his nose.

God wants David to take even more.

'WHO ... LOVES ... YA ... BABY?'

They've moved *Kojak* to Monday nights. He preferred it on Saturdays as his weekend treat but now the BBC have swapped it for *Cannon*. No catchphrase, no lollipop, instead the private dick Oliver Hardy with his beanbag gut, tufty hair, bouncer's moustache and shit theme tune. One less reason to stay in his caravan glued to the gogglebox with his frigid wife. One more good excuse to slip out into the fertile Cambridge night.

He's waited long enough. Four sexually agonising months since the last one. Seventeen whole weeks, each one's passing like the loosening of a grip – his on a town lulled into an increasing false sense of security that their bogeyman might have disappeared. The whole of Lent term without incident, even as the male student patrols that rallied to ward him off kept vigil in bedsitland, chivalrous knights in algae green polo necks, thick specs and CND badges. Their only mistake to keep watch by night and not day. While they were back in the library yawning over Chaucer, he was out in his van casing the very joints they think they're protecting, his little red notepad now a rapist's *Yellow Pages* of street names, house numbers, number of occupants, their names if he can find them on the electoral roll or stolen mail, whether they're especially young if he can gauge by the clothes in their wardrobe, sketches of floorplans, details of the door key and type of lock, all logged and entered with book-keeping precision using his own abbreviated code. But seventeen weeks is preparation enough. Easter term begins on Monday, and the late spring crop is rich for the reaping. Tonight, a new era of terror.

Saturday has ticked over into Sunday, Margaret already in bed when he quietly shuts the caravan door behind him, a black rubber torch in his hand as he creeps noiselessly across the field to his shed.

He gathers what he needs from his secret compartment beneath the floorboards. Two black plastic bags ready-packed with the tools of his trade. A nine-inch breadknife tied to a piece of cord to hang around his

SIMONGODDARD

neck. A sheath knife similarly taped to another makeshift lanyard. A bottle of ether and an ether pad. A couple of jemmies. Some wire clippers. A device made of an eight-inch rubber pipe with a socket attachment designed to fuse lights. A set of skeleton keys. A pair of black gloves made of imitation leather. Pink toilet tissues. An oil rag. A watch. His Allenburys Pastilles tin of papers and rolling tobacco. The rest, his disguises: several pairs of women's tights, underwear, make-up, dresses, shoes, a plastic hairbrush and numerous wigs.

Both bags will swing off the handlebars of the stolen blue-and-cream women's bicycle he'll ride into town, wearing a wig. Anyone seeing him will see a short, skirted person with long hair – in the dark, under the passing flash of a streetlamp or headlamp, what looks like a woman cyclist.

When he reaches the house of his chosen prey, he'll then change into his other costume. The one he's been designing these past seventeen weeks.

Leather. He's always loved it. A common enough fetish otherwise there wouldn't be money to be made in so many specialist magazines and blue films. There's even kinky shops you can go to catering for the creatively perverted. Masks, whips, patent spiked heels, rubber bondage hoods, latex bodysuits, like Selfridge's for S&M freaks. Though sadly none in Cambridge. There's only the Love Inn on Mill Road flogging the usual eight mill stag flicks, Swedish mags, dolls and dildos. But then he's a very enterprising little monster.

Hard for him to remember now what planted the seed. Any number of forgotten tremors over old copies of *Bizarre Life* and *AtomAge*. Or something he read more recently in a newspaper. Like monster envy.

Hardly a week passes when there isn't some new lead on the country's 'Public Enemy No. 1', wanted for a dozen masked raids and now four murders after a teenage heiress he kidnapped for ransom was found hanging naked in an underground drainage pipe. They call him 'the Black Panther'. Nobody's been able to identify him yet because any victims who've survived have only ever seen the wrong end of a double-barrel shotgun being pointed by a man in a black hood.

An old handbag does the trick. A big black one for carrying shopping, made of smooth hide and easy to mould. He trims it to fit his head, carefully measuring where to cut two big circular eyeholes like a

BOWIEODYSSEY**75**

Halloween pumpkin. Where it ends below the chin he sews on part of a ginger wig to look like a beard poking out: disguise upon disguise. For the mouth, he slashes a line where he sews on the chunky zip from the top of the same bag, allowing him to open and close it whenever he needs to speak. A bit like that weird orange glove puppet on children's TV.

For the Black Panther, a hood is a means of anonymity. But for him, something more. When he opens the bedroom door he doesn't want the girl to be in any doubt who he is and what he's about to do to her. It's like Batman. He never has to explain himself. The folk of Gotham take one look at his bat mask, bat cape and bat insignia on his chest and know exactly who they're dealing with. That's what he wants. The same trademarked infamy.

It's all in the finishing touches. A lick of white paint around the eyeholes, curving inwards like mean eyebrows. And then the forehead. So blank, so empty, it's calling out for it. A dozen thick strokes with his brush and he's done.

The first girl to see it is alone in her house in the early hours of Sunday morning when he breaks down her locked bedroom door, blinding her with a torch before switching on the light. Then she sees him properly.

A short man pressing a knife to her throat, dressed head to toe in black leather. That head a demonic superhero mask with zipped teeth gleaming like metal fangs, human eyes bulging from behind two peepholes and, above it, one word painted in chunky white letters. No introduction necessary.

RAPIST.

WEDNESDAY NIGHT, and you still can't switch on the TV for cops. Repeats of *Cannon*, and Burt Reynolds' *Dan August*, the last in the current series of *Baretta* and a new feature-length pilot about two hip young detectives in the fictional Bay City rolling around in baseball jackets and chunky knitwear.

In 637 Doheny Drive, David isn't watching *Starsky & Hutch*. The television is off. There is no music playing. All is deadly silent and even deadlier serious as he stands with both hands white-knuckling a lectern facing the indoor pool.

SIMONGODDARD

In front of him is an ominous bible-thick book on demonology compiled by Franciscan clergymen in the seventeenth century, its Latin title translating as *A Treasury of Terrible Exorcisms and Conjurations, the Most Efficient and Most Effective with Practical Proof, by Which Evil Spirits, Malevolent Demons and Everything About Human Bodies Besieged are Driven Out as with Scourges and Clubs.* Part of a shopping list he gave to Angie in preparation for this evening's heavyweight bout with the Prince of Darkness.

It's taken him a couple of weeks to work it out, but thanks to God and Freddie the dealer who've since told him repeatedly in so many lines, David now knows it for a holy fact.

Satan is living in his swimming pool.

Like every major problem in David's life, he's incapable of fixing it without Angie's help. Not that he expects her to get rid of the bastard all by herself, only to look after all the preliminary admin duties necessary to extract the Father of Lies from a chlorinated domestic leisure facility. Chiefly, the purchase of as many obscure volumes on diabolical pest control as the antiquarian bookshops of Los Angeles can supply and the trunk-call assistance of a white witch in New York City.

To meet Walli Elmlark is to behold a hippie Morticia Addams: a wardrobe that couldn't be blacker if it was handpicked by Henry Ford, neck garrotted by silver cosmic jewellery, inch-thick kohl outlining Gorgon eyes not unlike Peter Lorre's and an untidy jet-black bob thick enough to make several wigs in the same shape and style. A walking flashback to a joss-sticked yesterday of passing bongs to the squawk of *Nantucket Sleighride* when she could count on every progressive minstrel passing through Manhattan to bear a patient ear for her supernatural tongue and a hopeful eye on her superlative chest. That tongue ever eager to preach the neo-pagan mysteries of Wicca. 'The religion of the wise.'

Angie's first instinct is to employ the religion of the stupid, inviting the nearest Catholic priest to pop over and give Max von Sydow as good a run for his rosary as their shaky arms can muster. Only David refuses to let any stranger in the house should they turn out to be one of Beelzebub's foot soldiers in cunning disguise.

By process of elimination Walli is the only suitable sorceress of previous acquaintance, briefly crossing David's path back in the Ziggy summer

BOWIEODYSSEY75

of '72 when she flew to London to record a spoken-word album, still gathering dust having been judged unfit for sane society's consumption. Luckily, Angie still has the number of Walli's Upper East Side apartment, an equivalent Rentokil for anyone in need of advice on how best to rid their premises of the Horned Enemy of Mankind.

As Angie explains, their squatter problem carries some sense of urgency. As if having Lucifer paddling in their pool isn't enough, David is also of the three-ounce-a-week mind that his persistent foes, the witches of Los Angeles, have scheduled his death this Wednesday, 30 April. So-called 'Walpurgis Night', when practitioners of the dark arts are said to be at their most powerful. The same applying to the light arts of white witches like Walli, who tonight – the night in question – hangs on the other end of the telephone to lead David through her instructions like a spiritualist air-traffic controller, gently guiding him to salvation's runway as she pivots at the centre of a gigantic pentagram on her living-room floor.

David is first told to season the room with salt, garlic and a selection of fresh herbs. Not so different to preparing a Sunday roast.

He must then light blue candles, blue being the magick – with a k – colour of protection. Separate to any of Walli's essentials, but no less paramount, is the nearby billiard table, its surface scarred with enough chalky lines to look as if a big cat has clawed through the baize to expose a blank surface beneath. Each scratch like one of the Ten Commandments to be ingested nasally at regular intervals as battle fatigue demands.

The recited exorcism itself is left entirely to David and whatever jumbo he's chosen to mumbo from the *Thesaurus Exorcismorum*. Not being well versed in Ancient Latin, he picks a '*spiritus*' here, a '*sancti*' there, eyes blurring over the tightly packed letters with so many long Ss that look like Fs. He finds his own name, '*David*', his wife's, '*angeli*', and page after page of '*Exorcismus*' and '*Oratorio*', all of it blurted in short blasts like broken radio reception between sweating rushes to the billiard table while the blue candles softly burn.

And then a bubble.

A tiny plop on the surface of the pool as if blown by something below it. A fish. A frog. A person. Only the pool is empty.

David doesn't notice. Not until the second bubble. The first of many in quick succession like a kid with a straw blowing into their milkshake.

Then more. The bubbling swelling to a rolling simmer, the centre of the pool frothing wildly, now a jacuzzi on full power.

David clutches his crucifix.

'D–Domine – Deus om-omnipotens . . . '

Like a hell broth, boil and bubble.

'. . . nos–nostrum cujus fi–filius – *SNIFF!* – incarnus . . .'

Angie sees it too. Thinking her eyes are playing tricks, she retreats to the baize for some of David's smelling salts, then looks again. The same foaming white rapids.

'. . . f–f–fe vitem – *SNIFF!* – veram . . .'

Three time zones away in New York City, Walli the witch is spinning like a roulette wheel.

'. . . D–Deus – *SNIFF! SNIFF!* – er omnia! Secula secul–ul–ulorum!'

The tide suddenly surges.

'AMEN!'

Then just as suddenly stops.

'*SNIIIIIIIIIIFF!*'

IF IT WAS THERE BEFORE, nobody had ever noticed. David swears on his father's grave it wasn't. So does Angie, the only one brave enough to creep over to the edge of the now serene pool who sees it first. On the bottom, a large black mark as if it were scorched into the cement by something white-hot. Its shape, depending on where you stand, how you look at it, when you last slept and the chemical traffic of your major arteries, something like a horned beast. Possibly a demon. Maybe even *The* Devil.

But definitely a monster.

ELEVEN

EIGHT THOUSAND MILES APART, they fall simultaneously. The city of Saigon and the New York Dolls. As Operation Frequent Wind airlifts its last, as the final few hundred frightened Yanks claw their way onto the embassy rooftops smashing rifle butts in the faces of locals scrambling to beat them to one of the last lifeboat Chinooks, as they ignore the cries of desperate mothers holding babies over their heads begging them in broken English to save their child otherwise the Viet Cong will kill them, as they watch another surface-to-air missile blow up a distant Green Giant and all its crew, as the black smoke smothers the sky like an oil slick blocking out the sun, as the bars they drank in, cars they drove and apartments they called home are stripped and looted for anything of any worth in a city now worthless, as the People's Army close the gap and Big Minh unconditionally surrenders, in Florida, so does Malcolm.

He takes the Dolls as far as they can go. One thousand miles to the Sunshine State. Some of them don't even make it that far. Arthur souses out in South Carolina. Johnny and Jerry junk out not long after they hit Tampa, fly home, regroup and rename themselves the Heartbreakers before Saigon can switch to Ho Chi Minh City. That leaves Johansen and Sylvain to carry the leaky can for two last contracted gigs. It's over before it's over, but when the last chord fizzles it's well and truly *o-ver*.

One short tour of the South was as much as Malcolm could book them, his red patent leather life-support system packing up after three months without Minnie Riperton's America batting an eyelid. When he weighs up his losses, all he has left is a future blueprint of where he went wrong, a few stray notices describing the Dolls as *'the epitome of "punk rock"'* and a dose of the clap.

He also has the ever-faithful Sylvain, the first one to trust him and the last to leave him. Together they make the long drive back to New York via New Orleans, burning up gasoline and promises by the gallon, the highway lines like a runway launching Malcolm's thoughts home to London, where the same vagabonds hanging round SEX wait to needle him about their own group. Only now he has the know-how, as well as an unemployed Doll to bargain with. Which is when the solution to both their problems rushes towards him clear as the next Texaco truck stop.

Malcolm will return to England and prepare a new band using those same SEX kids. When they're ready, he'll wire Sylvain money for a one-way ticket to fly over and join them as their lead guitar player. With Malcolm's guile and a New York Doll in their midst they'll be sure to take no prisoners in a London begging to be resuscitated from the clubland sleeping gas of Jerry the Ferret and the Kursaal Flyers.

Sylvain is excited enough by Malcolm's plan to agree to the downpayment of his Fender Rhodes electric piano and his prized white Les Paul Custom stickered with wartime cheesecake pin-ups. Both spend the return flight rattling in a luggage hold 40,000 feet above the Atlantic while Malcolm's brain plots overtime in coach class.

The too eager SEX kids are there to greet him at Heathrow: Paul, the drummer, a skinny blond 18-year-old with the puffy eyes of a man twice his age; and Steve, the guitar player, who fancies himself enough to coif his hair like a model for C&A menswear.

The first thing Malcolm does is hand Sylvain's guitar over to Steve, who will take it to their band's next rehearsal, plugging it in to the amplifier he pilfered like the rest of their gear, most of it half-inched through the back door of the Hammersmith Odeon. Same as the microphones and bass amp he nicked two summers ago from David Bowie.

Thus the stolen stars align.

Malcom's shop in the King's Road is much as he left it save for the enriching vision of Jordan behind the counter, Vivienne's new designs on the rails and the fresh footprints of both Fleet Street and Scotland Yard. Something to do with some serial rapist in Cambridge. He struck again for the seventh time a few days ago and it's blown up in every tabloid, the biggest front-page story since the trial of that Yorkshire nutjob who asked for an exorcism because he thought he was Satan then went home and murdered his wife.

'WHO WILL STOP THIS MONSTER?'

It's not just the crimes but their execution. As the last two victims have described, he wears a black leather hood with the word 'RAPIST' painted on the forehead. It sounds a lot like the bondage hoods SEX sell, bought in from the London Leatherman in Battersea, a supply chain which led the men from the Met and the *Sunday Mirror* to beat a path to the door of number 430. They wanted to know how many hoods they've sold recently, and who to. The manager, Michael, told them all he could.

'I've sold a dozen hoods in eight months. I can't remember most of the people. But there was one chap who bought one a couple of months ago. He was short and dressed in a black leather jacket, dark trousers and black boots. He was carrying a motor-cyclist's helmet. Last week he came in again and bought a rubber hood with no eye slits and only a rubber tube to breathe through his mouth.'

The hysteria made last Sunday's *Mirror* cover splash. A giant picture of the SEX hood and the screaming headline: 'FACE OF THE RAPIST'.

This is Malcolm's welcome home to the land of Saint George. Sexually stifled realm of crashing sterling, Rod Hull and Emu and the seven-year-old number 1 sound of Tammy Wynette's 'Stand By Your Man'. He can smell it in the air like wet weather. Repression. Mediocrity. Hypocrisy. Conservatism.

And like a bop on the head from a copper's truncheon, he suddenly has an idea for a T-shirt.

TOM HAS TAKEN A MILLION PHOTOGRAPHS of a million stars but only ever gets asked about one. The picture he took 26 years ago this month in the same Seward Street studio where he shot Lana Turner,

Carole Lombard, Anita Ekberg and all the other nobodies nobody ever does ask him about. They just want to know about Marilyn. Wriggling naked under his lens upon a sea of red velvet in the panhandling summer of '49 when she needed the fifty bucks to stop her car being repossessed. She was embarrassed enough to sign his release 'Mona Monroe', hoping nobody would match the face on the naked calendar with the uncredited girl in the blue pinafore dress skipping out of church in *Scudda Hoo! Scudda Hay!* Four years later, and by the time she was sticking her hands in the cement outside Graumann's as the box-office sex bomb of *Gentlemen Prefer Blondes*, they had. Hugh Hefner reprinted it as the centrefold in the debut issue of *Playboy*, and while it didn't destroy her reputation, it made Tom's. All his classic portraits of the stars for Selznick and Goldwyn no longer meant diddly squat. From the moment he pressed that shutter, Tom became The Guy Who Took The Picture Of Marilyn's Tits.

It was a good picture too. Tom doesn't take bad ones. Give him a freckly alabaster Norma Jean and he'll light her smooth as a bronze nude on an art nouveau lamp.

'She looked just like a country bumpkin to me, but with the best figure I've ever seen.'

His job is to make the simply goodlooking look gorgeous and the simply gorgeous godlike.

'I think, out of all the women I photographed, Dolores del Río was the most perfect. The men, well, most of them were disappointing, with two exceptions. Clark Gable and Gary Cooper. These guys had charisma, on and off the screen.'

Possible exception number three steps into his studio's gallery-of-stars reception on the scheduled dot of 5 p.m. Minutes later they're sat in a make-up chair being prepared by a man named Jack whose brushes have previously tickled the cheekbones of Rita Hayworth.

David is in safe hands.

Today The Guy Who Took The Picture Of Marilyn's Tits is the guy in charge of David's new publicity shots. Tom photographs him just as he'd photograph anyone and anything, be it a head shot of Joan Crawford for Warners or an ad campaign for Squirt soda. His camera never lies, just exaggerates the truth, and David's doesn't need much exaggerating. The kind of face he hasn't photographed since Judy Garland fixed her nose.

BOWIE ODYSSEY 75

Atom-blasted by tungsten in crisp black-and-white – smoking a cigarette, reclining in a chair, reading a book, perched on the end of a bed – he's more deep-frozen handsome than ever.

The same applies to steaming-hot crazy, but Tom's professional interest stops at the epidermis. It's left to a magazine reporter covering the shoot to discover the ugly depths below the placid surface when she makes the mistake of trying to engage David in some light quotable conversation. He is brazenly aloof, foregoing charm for intellectual one-upmanship and vain self-analysis, quoting homo-superior chunks of Nietzsche.

'Although Bowie is a splendid visual subject,' she'll write, *'he is extremely trying and difficult to talk to. I found him an arrogant, narcissistic person and one wonders if this is an extension of his stage image or his real self.'*

She's right to wonder. This isn't David talking. It's the Duke.

The few journalists who've managed to interview him since he's been in LA have all had to contend with the Duke. A young kid from *Rolling Stone*, a woman from one of the British Sundays, an overseas call with an Australian rock mag. Each one hoping to talk to David Bowie about rock'n'roll and being David Bowie only to hear the Duke crack his whip and click his heels.

'I'd love to enter politics. I will one day. I'd adore to be Prime Minister. And, yes, I believe very strongly in fascism. Television is the most successful fascist, needless to say. Rock stars are fascists, too. Adolf Hitler was one of the first rock stars.'

The Duke. Fed on thin white powder and thinner white pages – on parallel universes and the evolution of the superman, the lost city of Atlantis and the Holy Grail, Kether the crown and Malkuth the king, the Golden Dawn and the Manson murders, human sacrifice and Heinrich Himmler – all scrunched up together in the wastebin of his head.

'You've got to have an extreme right front come up and sweep everything off its feet and tidy everything up. Then you can get a new form of liberalism. The best thing that can happen is for an extreme right government to come. It'll do something positive at least to cause the commotion in people and they'll either accept the dictatorship or get rid of it.'

The Duke. Picking the Wiener schnitzel from between his teeth with a Nazi eagle stick pin.

'I could have been Hitler in England. Wouldn't have been hard. Concerts alone got so enormously frightening that even the papers were saying, "This ain't rock music, this is bloody Hitler! Something must be done!" And they were right. It was awesome. Actually, I wonder? I think I might have been a bloody good Hitler. I'd be an excellent dictator. Very eccentric and quite mad.'

The Duke. Someone else's sick dream in a Brixton prison cell where the walls are bare and the nights are crystal.

LUST IS HIS DOWNFALL. It was always going to be. An addiction like any other. The anticipation before. The execution during. The satisfaction after. Not to mention the celebrity.

'Who loves ya, baby?'

Knocking Thatcher, the Rollers and even the *Sun*'s Top Television Actor Award winner Telly Savalas off the front pages. So many clippings he had to buy a second exercise book to stick them all in, each one suggesting he was still outwitting them. The only thing they got right was his height. They were looking for a man '5 ft 5 and under', except 'aged between 25–30', at least 16 years his junior. They'd assumed he'd bought his leather hood from some sex shop in London and were exhausting their resources tracking down customers. And if it wasn't the latest speculations on his psychological motives on page one – some even pinning it on the tired old *Clockwork Orange* copycat theory – it was another righteous bleat about a controversial ruling in the House of Lords. A new amendment to UK law where any man accused of rape who 'believed' the act was consensual must now be found not guilty. Open season for monsters.

Were it not for bad luck.

He had a skeleton key to the hostel and a floorplan of the corridors. He knew exactly which girl in exactly which room. He was even careful enough to choose a night before the new moon when the midnight sky would be at its blackest.

He just didn't count on the eels.

He should have. Slippery little fuckers emerging at night to hunt their prey, just like him. Hard to catch, too, unless you enjoy sitting in the pitch dark by the banks of the Cam at two in the morning waiting for your rod to twitch. Not many would, but best mates Ray and Harry were camped out in Grantchester Meadows for their third night on the trot, halfway through a bottle of scotch, nine eels already in the bag when the quietly burbling moonless peace was broken by a woman's scream.

Another thing he didn't count on. The screaming.

Usually they were too petrified to make a noise. This one went off like a burglar alarm. He'd knocked on her door in the dead of night, waking her up. She crept out of bed in her nightie and cautiously opened it on the safety chain. He tried to slash his way through with a knife, slicing her arm. That's when she started screaming. And didn't stop.

Screams. Eels. The freak variables he couldn't foresee.

The screams alerted the eel fishers, who rang the police, who caught him good as red-handed less than half a mile from the scene of the crime.

He couldn't have been more conspicuous. A short, sweaty little man in a red coat wearing a blonde wig, furiously pedalling a women's bicycle with two suspect plastic bags swinging off the handlebars, just a few hundred yards from an attempted rape gone 2 a.m. on an otherwise deserted Sunday morning. When they searched his belongings the first thing they pulled out was his homemade leather hood. They had him, sure as the eels in Ray and Harry's catch bag.

That was the early hours of yesterday. The day he lost his superpowers. The day the Cambridge Rapist died in the evidence room at Parkside station while he sat in his basement cell wondering what the wife was going to say.

'I'll always love you, no matter what.'

Poor Margaret. Poor stupid Margaret.

They drive him from the station to the courthouse in a yellow Ford van. He staggers out of the back handcuffed between two taller detectives, a trembling little toad, yanking one of their arms over his own as he tries to shield his face from photographers. The wrong kind of fame, the wrong kind of news clippings: even if he were free to do so, tomorrow's headlines won't be the sort he'd want to Pritt Stick in his scrapbook.

Cowering, head bowed, he doesn't see the hundreds of women pinned back by a line of police. Housewives, students, shop girls, office workers, all shaking fists and bellowing hatred. But he can hear them.

'BASTARD!'

'FILTHY PIG!'

'*HANG HIM!*'

The courtroom is packed. Chained between his captors, he slumps in the dock, his suit as grey as his complexion, his face cut and bruised from the fracas when they collared him, the gravity of shame dragging his head even further to the floor.

The clerk reads the charges.

Unlawful sexual intercourse with seven girls between last October and April, plus a further charge of attempted rape and another of causing grievous bodily harm.

The clerk asks him if he understands. He mumbles 'yes' without raising his head. He is sentenced on remand until the magistrates hearing in another eight days.

A decoy Black Maria keeps the raging mob baying at the wrong vehicle out front while they smuggle him through a side door and down a bicycle passage into a waiting panda car. A bit like being a pop star. Apart from the handcuffs.

The journey to Leicester Prison takes just under two hours. He makes it there in plenty of time to be processed before evening nosh, not that he's much of an appetite. It is Monday after all. Tonight, another new episode of *Koja*k goes out on BBC One. For the first time since it started, he won't be watching it.

TWELVE

THE LAND OF ENCHANTMENT. The cloudless sky like its cloudless people, wide-eyed and welcoming as their crystal clear lakes on a summer's day. The distant peaks of the Sangra de Cristo mountains biting up into a Hockney infinity of blue. Cactus trees, desert willows and ponderosa pines staking their claims in a gold rush of pale dusty earth. The daytime squeak of pinyon jays and the nightly choir of cicadas. David wishes all of America could be like this. Clean and pure.

New Mexico. Eight hundred miles from the portal to Hell in Doheny Drive he'll never see again. It's taken the grand irony of a movie to save him from the living death of Hollywood. With the eleventh-hour backing of British Lion distributors, the cameras are finally rolling on *The Man Who Fell to Earth*. Or, as the crew have taken to calling it, '*Bump*'.

David has spent the last three weeks in front of Mr Roeg's Panavision lenses consciously trying not to be himself while unconsciously giving the most convincing impression of David Bowie ever seen on screen. His days now have discipline and structure. Less time to lose his marbles worrying about warlocks or underlining more passages about Hitler in *The Spear of Destiny*. Early alarm calls and make-up chairs. Take after monotonous retake and touch-ups for continuity. Script revisions and camera blocking. Unsociable evenings learning the next day's scenes. None of it remotely rock'n'roll. Which makes him very happy.

SIMONGODDARD

And so does Corinne. His armour-plated vehicle in a cotton poplin dress, back where he needs her to fill the shoes Angie left when she flew back home; taking care of his daily business and, when necessary, opening fire on the enemy before she sees the whites of their eyes.

After David spent the first two weeks living in his trailer, refusing the comfort of the Albuquerque Hilton with the rest of the cast and crew, Corinne found him, and herself, a ten-room ranch house in the rattlesnaking hills near Santa Fe, complete with conservatory where David sets up his easel. When not on set he paints, he reads, he writes and continues taking what he must in order to maintain his focus on the job. For that he still needs what Mr Roeg would rather he didn't, however well he masks it.

His job, now, to be Thomas Newton. An extraterrestrial from an unspecified planet, not that it's significant. 'He could come from under the sea, or another dimension, or anywhere,' says David, who reads Newton as man in his purest form, polluted and brought down by the corruption around him. A visionary so destroyed by the ugliness of human suspicion, sex, greed and money that he's reduced to a tragic substance abuser making records to communicate how he feels. Art imitating life imitating art.

David's empathy for the role means he doesn't have to act. Just as well. The few scenes where he tries to are damning evidence of the fact he clearly can't. Even those don't especially matter. Mr Roeg thinks he's making a contemporary sci-fi drama about an alien visitor, but he isn't. *The Man Who Fell to Earth* is a feature-length documentary celebrating the physical beauty of David Bowie. An ever-so-softly pornographic love letter in 35mm Technicolor.

His face is Peter Pan smooth, like a porcelain sculpture where the artist made a virtue of having only a small amount of clay to work with: economically gorgeous with the minimum of milky skin and delicate bone. His crown jewel eyes close the ballot for next year's Oscar for Special Visual Effects. His hair, shimmering copper streaked with blond highlights, is the most luscious seen on screen since Grace Kelly's in *High Society*. There is no bad side for the camera to find. Lit from the left he is Garbo; from the right, Dietrich; front on, anything from a boyish Harold Lloyd to an entranced Conrad Veidt in *The Cabinet of Dr Caligari*.

A visage sharing an eternal luminosity with the brightest stars of the silent age. Except his is the curse to be cast in a talkie where such godlike perfection shatters in one burst of a Brixton vowel.

'Arthur, would you please slow down?'

Arthur being Newton's chauffeur, played by David's real-life driver and new bodyguard Tony Mascia, a former boxer from the Bronx who lasted 11 bouts, winning most on a knockout. He's also served three prison sentences. That was a long time ago, though, if circumstances demanded, you wouldn't put it past him to do what he had to and risk a fourth.

When the day's shooting wraps, Tony drives him back to his ranch in the same limousine that chauffeurs Newton in the film, David still wearing the clothes he wore on camera. Most of them were found ready on the peg by its English costume designer, May Routh, ex-girlfriend of *Aladdin Sane* photographer Duffy. Her choices including: the coolest duffel coat in the history of toggles in a rich loden green; soft Viyella shirts and others from Macy's boys' department; an all-in-one parachutist-style charcoal coverall; and a striking black suit in slub silk, the latter specially made for him by an LA fashion designer named Ola who looks like one of the Three Degrees and, it follows, has since joined David's Panini sticker book of lovers.

Every item is so exquisitely him he'll keep wearing them long after the shoot is over. Watching the rushes, Mr Roeg still deludes himself that with every day David penetrates further and further beneath the skin of Thomas Newton. Anyone can plainly see it's the other way around.

Unable to act with someone who doesn't, his co-stars rebound against him like a game of squash. None bounce harder than Candy Clark, best known for her Oscar-nominated role in *American Graffiti*, convincingly down-home as simple southern gal Mary Lou, David's on-screen love interest. She's also Mr Roeg's off-screen sex interest, though it doesn't stop him egging David on to writhe naked on a bed with her as the script demands while he looms over them pulling his focus. But then some scenes test David's acting ability a lot less than others.

Without Candy, he already has sweets enough. A posh and pretty 20 years old, heiress Sabrina Guinness, as in the drink, is cast in the film in an uncredited role as a student helping lecherous lecturer Rip Torn collect the papers he drops on the way to his car. David first met her in

Los Angeles where she was nanny to 11-year-old Oscar winner Tatum O'Neal. Evidently a great one. Tatum bought her a Porsche.

On a rare evening off, David takes Sabrina on his arm to the open-air opera house in Santa Fe to enjoy a sensual production of Bizet's *Carmen*. As its mezzo-soprano sings, love is a rebellious bird that no one can tame. And as David knows, lust is a ravenous dog and he holds the leash.

'Sex is very important. I've tried drugs. I try a new drug every time a new one comes out which is about once a year. But I never stay on it. It isn't necessary. Sex is, drugs aren't.'

Between takes, David's candour fills up the cassette of the man from the *Sunday Mirror*, flown over for an exclusive on-set report. The Duke fails to make an appearance and, for once, David is atypically open, talking about his life in the simplest and frankest terms.

He describes his childhood as 'unhappy', remembering his earliest home on Stansfield Road where his parents rented a room to a girl he later found out was a prostitute.

'I didn't get on with my mother, and my father, who is dead now, was a wonderful man and he had to stop the fights in the home. I was not lonely as a child but a loner. I still am.'

Without naming Terry, he mentions 'a relation five years older than I am' in a psychiatric institution.

'There is a streak of madness in the family. I thought I'd go mad myself once, that I'd just blow up like he did.'

Though he swears he doesn't need psychiatry himself.

'My act is my psychiatric couch. But I am not sure my audience understands everything I write. I certainly don't some of the time.'

This is David Jones speaking, not the usual Wowie Bowie flim-flam show. Call it the Newton effect. By giving him another character to play all day, he no longer has to act at being himself.

'I feel very strongly for Newton,' he confesses. And not that he needs to say it: 'He will stay with me for a very long time . . .'

THE WAY PEOPLE GO ON ABOUT IT, you'd think it was the only movie that had ever been made. The summer of '75 it may as well be. Like the motion picture equivalent of the moon landing or the assassination of

BOWIEODYSSEY75

JFK, everybody remembers where they were the first time they saw it and everybody's seeing it. Within six weeks of release an estimated eighth of the US population. You can't switch on a TV or radio without being bombarded by adverts for it. There hasn't been anything like this level of hype in all of Hollywood history. As one studio publicist puffs, 'This makes *Ben Hur*, *Cleopatra* and *Gone With the Wind* look in a different class!' Nobody saw it coming since it follows no cinematic trend. It's a monster movie like *King Kong*, a disaster movie like *Earthquake*, a horror movie like *Psycho*, a mismatched-couple-on-a-boat movie like *The African Queen* all rolled into one. Psychiatrists apportion its hysterical success to its basic appeal to humanity's primal fears. They said the same thing about *The Exorcist* but its 27-year-old director pinpoints the difference. 'The Exorcist made you vomit,' says Steven Spielberg. 'Jaws will make you clutch your hands to your armpits.'

Jaws. A funny name for a film. Based on Peter Benchley's best-selling book, but as movie titles go veering on the ever so slightly cryptic. Most films describe exactly what they're about. *The Exorcist* is about an exorcist. *The Godfather* is about a mafia godfather. *Love Story* is a love story. *Shampoo* is about a hairdresser. *The Towering Inferno* is about a big building that goes up in flames. None of these are *Times* crossword clues. Now and again you get something kooky like *American Graffiti* or *Paper Moon*, but they're the exceptions that prove the rule. Comedies are different; they can be *Duck Soup* or *What's Up, Doc?*, the audience doesn't care. Same with James Bond films. Call them *Diamondfinger* or *Live and Die Twice*, it makes no odds so long as that guitar starts twanging soon as the lights dim. But for the most part people like to know what they're in for. *The Longest Day* lasts three hours. Nobody's getting their money back.

Jaws is about a shark, but *Shark* isn't much of a title. Too blunt, too giveaway. Like if *Dirty Harry* had been named *Grumpy Cop*. Bad box office.

They might have called it *Panic on Amity Island*, or *The Great White Terror*, or *Nightmare Beach*, or *Deathswim*. All would have been fair warning of what goes down in *Jaws*. None would have been right.

Jaws works because it sounds rock'n'roll, like some scuzzy glam band from Staten Island. One word, one syllable, rolling off the tongue easy as a street drug or a bottle of soda. Smack. Coke. Jaws. Not a dishonest title either, just one removed from the uninspiringly obvious.

100

Why is everyone scared of the shark?

Because it's going to eat them.

How does it eat them?

With its fins?

No, dipshit, its fucking jaws!

There's your title. *Jaws* is perfect.

So is the film. Some movies are like a Swiss watch. Marvels of precise craftsmanship, everything in its right place, not a beat out of step. *The Man Who Fell to Earth* will never be that sort of film. It'll be weird and interesting and arty and provocative, but no one's going to be dropping their popcorn. It won't have that same *Casablanca* flawlessness *Jaws* has where you wouldn't change a thing, not even the ending when you can see the killer shark is really a hydraulically-operated 24-foot polyurethane model, the one the crew nicknamed 'Bruce'. No, *Jaws* is humungous for a very good reason.

Humungous doesn't even do it justice. *Jaws* is a national pandemic. One day everybody was going about their normal shark-free lives, the next all they can talk about is *Jaws*. It's like VE Day, Sputnik and The Beatles all at once. There's official *Jaws* T-shirts, *Jaws* bags, *Jaws* beach towels, *Jaws* pyjamas, *Jaws* plastic cups and *Jaws* rubber sharks, all selling by the thousand. Had Spielberg had his way there'd also be *Jaws* candy – a chocolate shark full of cherry-flavoured liquid that dripped like blood when you bit into it. The studio thought that was going too far but the unofficial merch goes even further. Ice cream vendors offering scoops of 'Finilla', 'Jawberry' and 'Sharklate' flavours, shark's teeth pendants, plastic shark fins to strap to the back while swimming. *Jaws* is a deep blue gold rush sinking its teeth into every crevice of American society like it was Ben Gardner's boat.

Time magazine splashes it on the cover the week of release. Every day some newspaper has yet another *Jaws*-spoofing political cartoon: the shark is Ronald Reagan, a Soviet submarine, a symbol of inflation, crime or political ambition, a feminist chewing lumps out of chauvinist pigs. Real estate ads in Pennsylvania show natural lakes with the guarantee 'No *Jaws* here!' Swimming pools get sassy by offering 'shark free lessons'. A discotheque on Long Island changes its name to Jaws and installs a stuffed shark beside the dancefloor. Fishermen who used to sell shark fins to restaurants are now selling jawbones to *Jaws* maniacs. One restaurant in Cape Cod adds broiled shark to its menu and trade is booming. Bob Hope jokes he's too scared to take a bath 'because my rubber duck keeps circling me'. Johnny Carson makes cracks about booking tickets to see it 'in the shallow end'. Others slap thighs over the one about Walt Disney making a special version for kids. 'Called *Gums*.' A novelty record is rushed out by Brooklyn producer Dickie Goodman called 'Mr Jaws', weaving a mock dialogue with the film's main characters out of snippets of contemporary pop hits. It is irredeemably awful. It reaches number 4.

This is what happens when a nation loses a war. While its soldiers limp home in bloody jigsaw pieces, its civilians queue round the block, again and again, to see people being eaten by a monster.

America is just that sort of country and 1975 is just that sort of year.

NEWTON IS ALMOST DONE WITH HIM, though he's not done with Newton. The last week of filming brings David near the Mexican border, to the national park of White Sands named after its 275 square miles of bleached desert. It's made of gypsum but looks exactly like a Sahara of purest cocaine. Like nowhere else on Earth, the reason David treads its dunes dressed as an alien for the scenes on his arid home planet. He wears a white skintight bodysuit and balaclava covered in a symmetrical webbing of clear plastic tubing stretching up over his head, its thick veins air-bubbling with water pumped by an aqualung-style backpack. A bald cap is smoothed over his scalp right down to cover his eyebrows, further dehumanised by the finishing touch of yellow cat's-eye contact lenses. He looks very obviously someone from another world, on another world. And yet he still looks unmistakably David Bowie: a strange-eyed, glycerine-skinned starman in cosmic threads. A Bowie the kids of '75 would still much rather him be than the soul boy next door of *Young Americans*. King of the Wackos.

At his most regally way out in the scene where Newton reveals his naked alien self to his lover Mary Lou. A plasticine-smooth body with no genitalia, a make-up process which takes four hours, beginning at 4 a.m. when David is still asleep, completed after he takes a last bladder-squeezing piss before they smooth over his groin ready for the long day's

SIMONGODDARD

shoot. No hair and no cock, and it still fails to stifle his radioactive on-screen Bowieness. Because nothing can.

By osmosing with the man who fell to Earth, Newton has bounced David back up into space. Where he belongs. Out there, floating in his tin can, waiting in the sky. He gave being an earthling his best Philadelphia shot, but there's no use in him pretending he's really just our Dave pulling birds down Samantha's on a Saturday night, twisting under the glitterball in his trendy wedge cut and Sta-Prest. A regular geezer. One of us.

He never was.

He's one of him. The only one. An outsider, a spook, an odd man out, an androgyn, a lone wolf, a dissident, a deviant, a partisan, a maverick, a stormy petrel, a loose screw, an irregular triangle in a world of squares.

He's not the Stylistics because if he was he'd have the UK's biggest-selling album of 1975. *Young Americans* won't even make the year-end Top 50.

No, because he's David Bowie. The whole point of David Bowie is to not be like everybody else. It's why the kids loved him and made him what he is. By being Bowie he let them know *they* were alright to not be like everybody else either. This is his purpose. An alchemist who turns the stigma of ostracism into the gold of individualism. The face and voice of the will-never-belong-and-thank-Christ-for-that. High priest of the Gospel of Otherness.

There is no one more other than Newton. The only species of his kind navigating an unfamiliar alien world. Reminding David of the singular thrill of being the only Bowie in town. A Bowie he thought he'd had to annihilate, unable to separate the pain of his fame from the awe of his art, believing the only way to prevent the former was to pervert the latter. Why *Young Americans* turned out his most reactionary album to date. A reaction against the name above the title, cutting off his nose just to spite the face of Defries and jump the putrefying sheep-pen of mid-Seventies rock'n'roll. To let the world know he isn't a Rod Stewart, Robert Plant, Roger Daltrey or any of the others with their shrieks and their beaks and their blues and their booze and their chests and their jets and their Jags and their shags. A one-man mutiny trying to define himself by what he isn't. But there are so many better ways. Ways he's always known.

Newton's law. The way of the weirdo.

That's what a David Bowie is. An Elvis from the outer limits making beautiful mysterious music for beautiful mysterious people. Always new, always different, always unsecondguessable, ripping up the rules and sticking them back together upside down and back to front. Always playing the sound of tomorrow's Bowie today.

The early hours of a Saturday morning find David in a grey bodysuit made out of the soft grey spongy material used to protect the inner casings of camera boxes. This is Newton, now an enigmatic celebrity billionaire, just returned from a test flight in the spacecraft he designed himself. Major Tom played by Major Tom.

The scene is shot at White Sands military base in the shadow of its 40-foot solar furnace. Among the hundreds of cheering extras made up of army personnel and their families is real-life *Apollo 13* astronaut Jim Lovell. As Newton is led by a police guard to his waiting limousine, the huge crowd of fans, press and photographers mob him as they would a rock'n'roll star. Struggling his way through their clamouring bodies, once safely in the car he instructs his driver to take him home.

Before the wheels roll an inch, David is already there.

THIRTEEN

SUMMER IS ALMOST OVER.

It crept in heehawing like a Blackpool donkey to 'Whispering Grass' as the government referendum on Europe saw Britons vote three-to-one to remain. It rubbed in the suncream in slow circular motions to 'I'm Not In Love' as the pound crashed to a record low. It sucked its Lord Toffingham lolly to 'Give A Little Love' as Roller Les McKeown was charged with causing death by dangerous driving after running over his 76-year-old neighbour. It splashed in the surf to 'Barbados' as tripefleshed Englishmen boiled alive in a 90 Fahrenheit heatwave. And now, in the last Mateus-pink sunset of August, it drowns the end-of-holiday blues to 'Can't Give You Anything (But My Love)'. A song plucked from the candy floss of cloud nine about an ordinary guy whose pockets are empty. Danced to by ordinary guys and girls whose pockets aren't jingling any louder.

The only ones whose are empty them in the Commons bar, including Wilson's cabinet who've sat counting their pay rise and sucking their briars while inflation leaps a Mother Hubbard 25 per cent.

The working class are now the survivor class with three and a half million families hanging out to dry on the poverty line. Another half a million have already lost the will to cling on, hunger no longer a pang but a terminal illness. Labour's winning manifesto promised 'to protect the poor' and 'to maintain and improve their living standard'. All they've given them is a slow malnutritious death by beans on toast.

The late summer nights shorten and the dole queues lengthen. Now a record one and a quarter million out of work. The ones joining at the back aren't long out of school blazers, their whole puberty wasted on education when the only thing 'Sir' need ever have taught them was how to sign their giro. Youth unemployment is at its worst since the war, the most desperate feeling they've no choice but join the army and pray there isn't another this side of Christmas. While Labour employment minister Michael Foot snores in his mothballs, it takes his Tory shadow opposite to flag the crisis in the House. 'This is a social situation which should not be tolerated,' warns the member for Lowestoft. 'It can lead to delinquency and moral degradation and a legacy of deep recession such as we are beginning to see can remain for ever.' A sentiment echoed by an exasperated careers officer in Liverpool. 'How can you blame youngsters for rebelling and turning to vandalism in a society which teaches them up to the age of 16 and then throws them on the scrapheap?'

How can they blame them?

Ah, but they do. The last football season witnessed ashen-faced coppers picking 'kung fu stars' out of their helmets – many homemade by kids in metalwork class – trains set alight and fans pissing into the electronic scoreboard in the FA Cup final. This one kicks off with 270 arrests and 16 stabbings. Thus the beautiful game shifts from the back page to the front for all the wrong reasons. 'I would like to see these hooligans birched,' seethes referee Eric Read. 'What is really horrifying is that there seem to be a lot of young girls involved. They appear to be bringing hysteria to the world of football. We live in a very difficult world.'

A world twice as difficult if you're the bored belittled boracic young for whom fashion is the preposterous magazine fantasy of a 'must-have' glittery Silver Surfer T-shirt costing £8.50 – leaving all of 10p change from a week's dole.

Affordable glamour has since died and gone to hell in Kensington High Street, where the zombies of style scavenge the cold carcass of a too-recent yesterday. Like some once immortal screen goddess cruelly disfigured in a car accident being wheeled before her public in all her shameful ugliness, so Big Biba breaks the heart of all who ever adored her. It is the beast of cutthroat capitalism that kills the beauty of Barbara Hulanicki's dream, the company shareholders who replaced her with the men in grey suits, who replaced Biba's palatial splendour with pile-'em-high squalor. The last few weeks of its closing-down sale couldn't look any worse had the IRA bombed it: whole floors either closed or mid-demolition, giant mounds of cut-price clothes and hats dumped on the ground to be pecked at by desperate bargain hunters like seagulls on a rubbish tip. By New Year it will reopen as another branch of Marks & Spencer and the last echo of its glorious giraffe-print pretensions will be silenced by the death groan of crimplene conformity.

It is no longer acceptable to be exceptional. As ill-judged a time as any for Mary Quant to bring out her first official range of 'make-up for men'. Not in this post-glam age of the cheeky chappie when the new archetype of English machismo is strawberry blond Jagger-faced shagger Robin Askwith. *Confessions of a Pop Performer*, his second film dimpling his buttocks as human toilet plunger Timothy Lea has just hit screens like a rotten tomato. The first one about a *Window Cleaner* broke domestic box-office records, and a third about a *Driving Instructor* is already in production. The profession doesn't matter so long as the audience of honking sea lions get their tally of tit and fanny and the gags remain exactly the same. In this one, set as they all are in what looks like a badly preserved suburban 1969, Askwith drums with a band called Kipper. In one scene he walks into a record shop to buy a copy of his own single. The saucy girl behind the till informs him it's out of stock.

Askwith: 'Do you think you'll have it in again?'

Saucy shopgirl: 'I wouldn't be surprised.'

They then proceed to have roly-poly sex behind the counter to an ever-changing soundtrack including Spike Milligan's 'On The Ning Nang Nong'. In skint and starving England there isn't much else to laugh about.

No jokes, no clothes, no cash, no hope.

The horror story of this summer's teenage runaway documentary *Johnny Go Home* may have created another moral outcry in the tabloids but it hasn't stopped virgin meat piling into the capital every day to be racked out afresh on the Dilly. Kids as young as 12 can buy smack for three quid out of the fiver they earned tossing off a grandad, leaving them more than enough for a 30p grotburger from Maltese Joe and a ticket to the nearby Odeon to shoot up in the backseats of *Rollerball*. Here's your future, kids. The world as one big corporate hell by the year 2018, when unthinking society will be kept in its place by an ultraviolent spectator sport like a cross between speedway, American football and the private fantasies of the Marquis de Sade. The aim of the game: 'To demonstrate the futility of individual effort.'

The future?

There is no future.

There is only a monster from outer space treading westward down the King's Road on a Saturday afternoon. Or that's how it looks to his fellow pedestrians. His hair dyed cucumber green, wearing a tatty Pink Floyd T-shirt held together with safety pins and customised with the words 'I HATE' painted along the top. Walking against the tide of time and place as he passes the tired hoarding for *Rocky Horror*, nostrils flaring to the street aroma of diesel and cigarettes with top notes of sweet and sour from Bamboo Kitchen. The road beginning to curve, just before the Asterix creperie, he crosses to the opposite side. Almost at the World's End, and in a few short strides his journey's.

It's not the first time he's stepped over the threshold of number 430. He's been before with his mates, all, like him, named John, including the hopeless Bowie wannabe who first brought them here: confusingly born a 'Simon' and latterly getting used to his new nickname 'Sid'. Not with him today, though another John is on hand to help him find his dream pair of white suede brothel creepers.

He's out of luck. The shop still sells stray Teddy Boy bits and bobs, but it's now mostly patent leather, rubberwear and screenprinted T-shirts. Like the one with a drawing of two cowboys face-to-face, naked from the waist down, their swollen cocks touching between them. Or the new one he hasn't seen till today, a photo of a leather fetish hood overprinted with the words 'CAMBRIDGE RAPIST'.

Top lip jutting, he skims through the rails of heavy-duty latex gloves, silver lamé suspender belts, a gold peephole bra with crotchless knickers and a peach rubber négligée, absent in his own thoughts and the jukebox ruckus of 'Psychotic Reaction'. Not expecting anyone to pop him a question.

'Oi. Can you sing?'

Yes, summer is almost over.

For now comes the winter of the discontents.

FOURTEEN

'*FAHREN, FAHREN, FAHREN . . .*'

David is driving, driving, driving. His body sat cross-legged on a carpet in Bel Air, his head speeding white lines down the centre of a German motorway.

'*Fahren, fahren, fahren . . .*'

His windscreen is a pair of speakers, his dashboard his stereo, the petrol in his tank an album that's already been in and out of the Top 5 in America and the UK months ago when David was otherwise busy fermenting urine and wrestling Mephistopheles. But now it's on his turntable and rarely off it. A record with no obvious antecedent other than 'Popcorn' by Hot Butter and the pocket calculator burps soundtracking *Doctor Who*, albeit more tuneful than both. No rock, no roll, just pulse'n'beep. The sort of music that might exist on Newton's home planet, synthetic and futuristic, algorithmed and microchipped, a sensual human experience fabricated by something audibly non-human, even if its creators are four Herren of Fleisch und Blut from Düsseldorf.

'Not a musical town,' they say, 'and ve are not part of a musical movement. And more than movements in music ve are rather more aware of ze more spiritual movements in general, in art or psychology, science and, of course, general technology. Ve are not part of ze musical world.'

109

BOWIEODYSSEY75

David loves Kraftwerk all the more for it. Driving, driving, driving at 33⅓, *Autobahn* is his new music for night and day.

Now he's back in Los Angeles, they're one and the same again. He returned to the city like a bad habit and soon as he arrived resumed all his others. They found him again quicker than he found them. His first week back, good old Ron hauled him to a party in Beverly Hills for another Englishman in exile with a headful of sherbet. Actor, Goon and sociopath Peter Sellers is also the inventor of a vodka-based cocktail he describes as 'a delicious white sea of snow'. He calls it 'You've Made An Old Man Very Happy'. Surviving eight heart attacks before he was 40, he should know. Probably why he celebrated his 50th like he was chasing double figures. To make it there as quickly as possible he invited every rock musician in town with an itchy snitch and a British passport, including Keith Moon, Joe Cocker, Bill Wyman and good old Ron, who roped David into joining them in the evening's live entertainment as saxophonist in their makeshift blues group, Trading Faces. Marty Feldman played drums while Clouseau the birthday boy and Peter Cook took turns out-funnying one another on vocals over the unrehearsed blizzard. It sounded a lot like the film Sellers starts shooting next month: *Murder by Death*. Cary Grant even stopped by to say hello, the night passing much like a few rounds of You've Made An Old Man Very Happy. A delicious white sea of snow.

David's latest rented home, which feels anything but, is a dark and vibeless mock-Tudor house on Stone Canyon Road, chosen by Corinne, who savours the oxygen Angie isn't around to breathe by installing herself as combined secretary, governess and wet nurse. She buys his groceries. She fields his calls. She finds him lying unconscious and checks he hasn't overdosed by holding his chopping mirror next to his mouth to make sure he's still breathing. She does what she must so she too becomes a daily fix David cannot function without.

His one salvation is work. Now that Mr Roeg's cameras have stopped rolling he is not without purpose. The papers have already been speculating on his next movie role, wild rumours not worth the salt on the chips they're wrapping that he'll be starring in a biopic of Frank Sinatra or Rudolph Valentino, or even an Italian spaghetti western. But in all the far-fetched tinsel talk they're forgetting his day job, the one that's been clogging up the airwaves of every station from Tacoma to Tallahassee for the past two months.

While David's been away pretending to fall out of the sky, so has the US hit he's always wanted but long given up on. 'Fame', the record he cut with John back in January about how much he loathed being a pop star. Released as a single in the boogie number 1 summer of 'The Hustle', 'Jive Talkin'' and 'Get Down Tonight', its 4/4 pimp strut finds David in perfect simpatico with the sexy swing of young American hips. It's currently rear-bumping the Isleys' 'Fight The Power' at number 5 and on course for a six-gun shootout with 'Rhinestone Cowboy' before the end of September. 'Fame' has only made David even more loathsomely famous. And Defries more loathsomely rich.

Smelling similar pay dirt, RCA want to squeeze new music out of David as fast as he'll bleed it. Liberated by Newton, his inner screwball is ready to open up his veins again.

Plans have been put in place for his return to the stage in 1976 with a world tour obliging a new album to coincide. One to take immediate priority over the separate soundtrack to *The Man Who Fell to Earth* he's promised Mr Roeg, so far half-sketched and being redrawn daily every time the needle lifts after another spin of *Autobahn*.

Never having made an album in Los Angeles before, David sees no reason why he should start now. His musicians are all in New York. So is his last producer, Harry. So is the studio where he cut 'Fame', Electric Lady. This is what he wants, the same magic formula. Trusted faces in a trusted place.

Except for one snag. His musicians are free. So's Harry.

Electric Lady isn't.

'We can't get in,' Harry tells him over the phone. 'It's booked solid the whole of September.'

At the end of the line, David deflates. So punctured, it doesn't even cross his mind to ask the obvious question.

'Booked solid by who?'

HAS EVER A MORE ELECTRIC LADY walked into Electric Lady? If you told her this was where Bowie cut 'Fame', it'd mean nothing to her. Far as she's concerned, this is Jimi's place and anyone else who ever sets foot in it is just a no-good interloper. That would include her, too, had she not the royal pardon of having met his Purple Haziness here outside on the sidewalk the night it opened in August 1970. The cinema next door was playing *Rider in the Rain* and the wind cried Mary. Her, then an aspiring poet in a gawky straw hat, aged 23; Jimi, a stone free spaceman with 91 days till he turned 28 but just 22 till he'd die at 27. He told her he wanted his studio to be somewhere musicians from all over the world would gather to play the universal language of peace. He asked if she digged. She dug, but that was five years ago and now's no longer the time for flowers in anyone's hair. Patti's come to Jimi's temple to kick up a war dance.

Not that she doesn't still believe in peace. Patti has the daisy-chained heart of a hippie but the mouth of a banshee. Lips of barbed wire and a tongue like a flaming torch. She's Joan of Arc played by Marlon Brando: on paper her words say, 'I am not afraid', but the grit of her voice snarls, 'What've you got?' She will burn at the stake as she spits in your eye, burn for her belief in the liberating bliss of rock'n'roll as something worth dying for. The very thing David has forsaken because he thinks it's finished, because he thinks too much, because when he listens to rock'n'roll he only listens with his head. Patti's ears are in her guts; that's why her every song is a body blow. She sings like she's running to jump off a cliff with no regard for how high the drop and won't stop singing till she breaks her neck. Sometimes she smashes on the rocks below, broken-boned but still alive, staggering to her feet to limp back up and hurl herself off all over again. She is fearlessness personified. Albeit in the body of an undernourished crow.

Patti will be here for five weeks in Electric Lady, working midnight to six in the morning, some days five in the morning till lunch with the same four-piece band Dylan checked out when he caught her back in June at The Other End, twirling on stage in her Keith Richards T-shirt like a treaty between the battle of the sexes. They include guitarist Lenny Kaye, who in his daylight capacity as a freelance rock hack was part of the US junket flown over to review David play Aylesbury in the Ziggyfied summer of '72. Television's Tom Verlaine will also pop in as required to pull thorns from the paw of a bleeding Jazzmaster, while the producer is John Cale, formerly from the black hills of Carmarthenshire, formerly of the Velvet Underground, formerly part-responsible for the greatest debut album ever to come out of New York City. Until this one.

She'll call it *Horses*. It suits it. Wild mustang music of untameable beauty. Not every song is a stampede, but fast or slow each note gallops free as her voice, a paragraph that doesn't stop at the end of the page, spilling off into the Kerouac depths of dimensionless space. No word obvious, some of them opaque, all of them true.

Six months ago Patti told a journalist, 'I don't want to do a record unless it's fantastic and will really do something to people.' This is, and this will, and this is the reason why David is unable to return to Electric Lady to make his new album. Because Patti Smith is here instead, town-crying *'do the Watusi!'* as the elflike star maidens on the wall strip off and change course for the heart of the sun.

They do not miss him.

PATTI'S STILL THERE on the anniversary of Jimi's death, the day she records her 'Elegie' to him, the same day David, long since resigned to his fate as a prisoner of Los Angeles and all its hollow gestures, appears as a guest on America's most-watched TV variety show. A statistic the producers of *Cher* trumpet as loud as they can, even knowing as they do when his episode finally airs on a Sunday evening in late November, that week, as every week, most households will be watching *The Six Million Dollar Man* instead.

It's Cher's second solo season after the regrettable cancellation of her and her husband's ratings-busting *Sonny & Cher Comedy Hour*. They would have continued but for the small matter of a $10 million divorce petition. Sonny was first to change networks and launch his own *Sonny Comedy Revue*. It ran for 13 weeks before being cancelled.

Cher has been a lot luckier in television, less so in love. Four days after her and Sonny's decree absolute, she married Southern rocker Gregg Allman of the Allman Brothers. He'd been a guest on her show a few weeks earlier when they duetted on 'Don't Mess Up A Good Thing'. Pity Gregg never heard a word. Cher's second divorce petition hit his doormat nine days after they cut the cake. Maybe the fact Gregg passed out in the toilet after taking heroin on their first date should have been a warning sign. Cher was nothing if not pragmatic.

'I've always believed it best to admit one's mistakes as quickly as possible.'

BOWIE ODYSSEY 75

There's not much that fazes Cher. She can marry a junkie on Tuesday, ditch him on Wednesday and still be camera-ready Thursday looking like Pocahontas in Vegas, not a sparkle out of place. The sky could collapse and Cher would blink her roller-blind lids, step over the rubble and la-di-da into another chorus of 'The Beat Goes On'. Her eyes are a pair of hieroglyphics, the kind of eyes that don't require her to speak unless she has to. She loves you, she hates you, she thinks you're an imbecile. Gaze into those crystal balls and you'll know without ever having to ask.

At the age of 29, Cher fully understands life is ridiculous, which is why she lives in a mansion the size of Windsor Castle with her 1,000 dresses and 500 pairs of shoes. You can tell by the way she sings, like low honking laughter to a tasteless joke. The minority who don't want to watch Steve Austin on a Sunday night aren't dumb. Monday's coming like an occupying army but – rejoice! – here's Cher dressed like someone's tried to make a Christmas tree out of Cleopatra's needle, wailing '(I Can't Get No) Satisfaction'. The world really ain't so bad. La-di-da-di-da.

David arrives at the CBS studio in Fairfax looking like Newton. That is a non-member of the human race desperately trying to pass himself off as a regular Joe in a suit from Sears Roebuck, let down only by the colour of his hair and a face transmitting its insanity loud as the RKO Radio Pictures mast. Cher reads the airwaves. David is obviously out of his mind, and she's cool with it. She's said 'I do' to worse. They flirt, naturally, but then last week Cher's guest was Kermit the Frog. She flirted with him too.

Besides the crew, there is no live audience for what would otherwise be David's first public performance of the year. He takes no part in the show's routine comedy skits, though his three performances are funny ha-ha enough.

He sings 'Fame' to a backing track as if a strong antipsychotic sedative is either taking effect or wearing off, most of it like it's someone else's song he agreed to do but for the life of him can't remember why.

For the *Young Americans* ballad 'Can You Hear Me' he's joined by Cher, a psychedelic Una Stubbs in wifey black bob and sequined butterfly frock. His blow eyes glittering, his mandible grinding, David's is a heavyweight Don Juan croon swinging for a knockout but Cher's kemosabe squall makes it an even bout, duetting with old-hand 'I Got You Babe' muscle memory. As modern pop couples go they're hands down sexier than Captain & Tennille.

The final number with the house band is a medley that starts and ends in 'Young Americans' but for its middle flab changes tune with the impatience of a grouchy grandma with a remote control zapping from channel to channel, satisfied with none. David, never plainer in grey tweed jacket and pleated white slacks, the Thin White Duke retiring to the golf club for the stiffest of G&Ts. Cher, never stranger in a short white toggled poncho and fat red wig like a topiaried hedge on a palace lawn. Together, hamming and hollering from song to song like it's a game of snap. 'Young Americans' batters into Neil Diamond's 'Song Sung Blue', hammers into Three Dog Night's 'One', prangs into the Crystals' 'Da Doo Ron Ron', slams into the Fifth Dimension's 'Wedding Bell Blues', bulldozes into the Chantels' 'Maybe', skids into Buddy Holly's 'Maybe Baby', piledrives into The Beatles' 'Day Tripper', heaves into the Marcels' 'Blue Moon', skewers into the Platters' 'Only You', bayonets into the old Bing Crosby standard 'Temptation', slugs into Bill Withers' 'Ain't No Sunshine', tramples into the Coasters' 'Young Blood', car crashes back into 'Young Americans' again, all 14 transitions whizzing by in less than four breathless minutes. It's primetime musical schizophrenia, which suits David's attention span just fine. Cher, too, looks as if she hasn't had this much fun since the divorce judge ordered Sonny to reimburse her legal fees.

Over on the saner turf of ABC, the Bionic Man will be breaking up a moonshine gang in Georgia and most of sofa-beached America will be cheering him on. While on Cher-shaped CBS, worlds collide and stars collapse in a black hole of light entertainment sucking the Seventies in on itself like a gurgling plughole. If you never saw, it never happened.

SHE COMES IN PEACE TO START A WAR. Not with their country but her own. She comes the week 'Fame' reaches number 1 with a suitcase of new clothes to impress the New World. Soft fabrics, fresh pastel shades of turquoise and emerald, high necklines and frills, voile evening dresses with a Victorian feel.

A whole new Maggie.

BOWIEODYSSEY75

Most of the outfits for her first American trip were made to order by 35-year-old German designer Ilian Balfour, sparing Maggie the blushes of visiting his studio stuffed between the knocking shops of Soho by taking his tape measure to her Chelsea home.

'I wanted to give her a casual elegant look within the framework of what a politician can wear,' swoons Ilian. 'I can't put her over as too glamorous, but I want to make her look softer and more feminine, not that cardboard stiff gabardine. I think that Mrs Thatcher is tired of her fuddy-duddy matronly image. I think she has a beautiful face, a lovely smile and a very good figure. I want to get her slender look across.'

Ilian does slender very well. His other clients include the disco waitresses at the Intercontinental hotel and Mick Jagger. This is how much Maggie's world has changed in the six months since she became leader of the Opposition. She's now a waxwork in Madame Tussauds. Photographed by David Bailey for *Vogue*. Sharing a clothes designer with a Rolling Stone. By the end of the week she'll also have met President Ford in the Oval Office and sat on the NBC *Today* sofa opposite Barbara Walters. Barbara will ask her if she thinks she'll be the next UK prime minister. Maggie will answer, 'I believe so.'

For her first major speech in New York's St Regis Hotel she opts for a black see-through chiffon dress, finely pleated with a satin-trimmed waist. It's not one of Ilian's but an old favourite she's had for three years. When he sees the photos in tomorrow's papers he'll despair.

'*That* is not my dress *at all*. She looks *huge!*'

And when Maggie returns to England she'll abruptly dispense with his services.

But first she dispenses with the rest of Wilson's bronchial Britain. War is declared at 8 p.m. to the assembled diners of the Institute of Socioeconomic Studies including various senators, governors, mayors, clergymen and the chairman of Ford Motors. Cobwebbed Westminster etiquette dictates politicians must never criticise dear Old Blighty during public engagements abroad. That sort of vulgar behaviour just isn't cricket. Except this is Maggie, this is America and tonight she's playing rollerball.

'The pursuit of equality.'

What she claims is the problem. The soggy liberal belief that every base lackey peasant is entitled to the same as the landed gentry. That the poor should be rich and the rich should be poor. Pshaw and pshaw!

116

'I think we have very much now come to the end of the road,' she warns. 'What is more desirable and more practicable than the pursuit of equality is the pursuit of equality of opportunity, and opportunity means nothing unless it includes the right to be *un*equal. The relentless pursuit of equality has damaged our economy in a variety of ways. It's not the sole cause of what some have termed the "British sickness", but it is a major one.'

And lands herself straight on the front page of tomorrow's *Sun*.

'THE BRITISH SICKNESS – BY MAGGIE. AN ASTONISHING SPEECH IN U.S.'

It sure is.

Some animals are more equal than others.

Astonishing.

FIFTEEN

THE MOUNTAIN COMES TO MUHAMMAD. Everything David wants from New York City flies the best part of 3,000 miles to join him in LA. The 'Fame' band of Carlos, Earl and Dennis with a new bass player, George. The 'Fame' producer, Harry. Everything except the 'Fame' studio.

Its substitute is Cherokee in West Hollywood, the recently revamped MGM Recording Studios where Judy Garland decided 'There's No Business Like Show Business' and Sammy Davis Jr sugared 'The Candy Man'. David supplies his own bonbons, scattering them around Studio 1 like a Woolies Pic'n'Mix. A fat white heap on the mixing desk. The same on top of the piano. Another on the music stand in the vocal booth. As many as he needs to hop room to room from one to the other like sniffing stones. Harry and the band sniff with him as required to keep pace with his sleepless industry, open 24 hours, same as the studio bar. An industry all the more bamboozling since David doesn't seem to have any idea what it is he's actually recording.

They have an album to make but next to no songs. David turns up on day one with just one – a cute doo-wop-ish tune called 'Golden Years' with secondhand chords swiped from the Drifters' 'On Broadway' – itself a two-year-old hangover from the title track of *Aladdin Sane* and a riff so universal, right now in Electric Lady Patti Smith is using the same two-step interval on Van Morrison's 'Gloria'.

Like a quick spray job on a stolen car, the band disguise it the same way they disguised 'Foot Stompin'' as 'Fame', liquefying the tempo to a sweet disco froth, only much smoother. 'Fame' is a hard cube of right-angles: 'Golden Years', a shiny sphere of curved edges. 'Fame' is an angry swagger: 'Golden Years', a sexy sashay. 'Fame' is a song of hate: 'Golden Years', a song of love. Self-love. Its words may offer a helping hand, but 'Golden Years' is a Saturday night super swank, an explosion of self-confidence like the first hit of cocaine. It's David Bowie showing off how fantastic it feels to be David Bowie, bouncing his voice from low to high with turtle-waxed ease, one moment low smoochy Elvis, the next cloudsurfing with Frankie Valli. A song that looks itself in the mirror, cocks an eyebrow and blows a kiss. The neon lights are bright and the town is yours in a world where there is no such thing as Monday morning. There's just you, your new shoes, the night and the dancefloor. You will not be going home alone, and when you do you'll peel off your clothes *very* slowly, whistling just like David in the outro. And the sex, of course, will be off-the-Richter amazing.

'Nothing's gonna touch you.'

It can't. 'Golden Years' is invincible.

As the only new song David has for the album, it's also completed remarkably fast.

The rest of it won't be.

SEEDS SCATTER AND CONKERS FALL. The sycamores of England turn a rich maroon, the cherries a lipstick scarlet, the planes a coffee brown, the birches a biscuit yellow and the 'Sailing' September of Stewart becomes the 'Hold Me Close' October of Essex.

The new songs, mostly love songs, bob like lost messages in bottles on a choppy sea of old songs. Today's news still yesterday's papers, crinkly and brown as the autumn leaves. Art Garfunkel coos 'I Only Have Eyes For You'. Roger Whittaker dribbles 'The Last Farewell'. Showaddywaddy hiccup Buddy's 'Heartbeat' only three months after a couple of hundred Teds assembled in the Old Kent Road to witness the ritual burning of the Waddy's previous shooby through Eddie's 'Three Steps To Heaven'; nothing personal, they did the same to Mud's 'Oh, Boy!'. The Mayfair

BOWIEODYSSEY75

offices of RCA UK issue five more singles in their occasional 'Maximillion' series of 'three golden oldies for the price of two' retailing at just 59p. This batch includes bygone warblers Elvis Presley, Perry Como, Hank Locklin and Middle of the Road in the unlikely company of David Bowie. His chosen antique is 'Space Oddity', his first Top 5 hit six years ago in 1969. So old that most of the papers don't bother reviewing it, except for *Record Mirror* and the very complimentary celebrity guest critic in *Sounds*.

'I think it's a great record. I liked it when I heard it all those years ago. The whole production of the record is very, very professional and this time, who knows, it could get right up to the top. I mean, it deserves to because it's a very well-made record. It makes you listen and it's clear. I would like to sneak in at the back of one of his concerts but it would be awkward for me to just sit in the audience because they'd say, "What's he doing, Father Christmas!" I hear David Bowie is a great showman, and good luck to him again with this.'

Thank you, Bruce Forsyth. Didn't he do well?

If they're not old songs, they're silly songs. Carl Malcolm's chubby lovin' 'Fattie Bum-Bum', Jasper Carrott roid-roid-roiding his 'Funky Moped' and two versions of 'Una Paloma Blanca' hokey-cokeying their way into the Top 10. All the evidence anyone needs that Britain is the halfwit of Europe.

But there are cleverer jokes yet to be cracked, and in a studio in Whitechapel they're cracking in fandangos. Danny La Rue rockers Queen spend lost lifetimes rushing to finish their new single scheduled later this month. It's six minutes long, sounds like *The Pirates of Penzance* as performed by Sweet and staggers under the Lisztian expectations of 'Bohemian Rhapsody'. Jumbo-choppered frontman Freddie – rock'n'roll's unsolicited answer to Dick Emery's vicar – pledges if necessary to work round the clock to meet the label's deadline. 'I'll sing until my throat is like a vulture's crotch.' And he will, dears, he will.

But Bismillah and Beelzebub? This is just fantasy.

The sound of real life is Chelsea hooligans smashing shop windows on Fulham Road following their 2–0 defeat to the Cottagers. The last breath of an 11-year-old boy from Tyneside sniffing himself to death with a tin of Evo-Stik. The patter of drizzle upon the roof of Norwich Crown Court and, below, a gavel banging like a clap of thunder – hammering a full stop in the story of the Cambridge Rapist.

120

It ends with all the fame he could ever have wished for, his face all over the weekend's papers, front and insides. His real face, stripped of any exotic disguise, mean and pitiless. Along with his real name.

Peter Samuel Cook.

The ugly little man behind the leather mask, now cringing in the stark white courtroom, his dark hair grown out after four months on remand, a stubby, emotionless figure in a grey check suit with a white handkerchief in the breast pocket, mauve shirt and blue tie.

His father will tell reporters he'd have rather his son had committed murder. His wife will weep remorse and sob how it all started with 'a rape episode' of *Kojak*. 'That programme certainly gave him the idea to do the rapes,' she'll swear. 'He was fanatical about the show. He never missed an episode.' Even though the closest thing to 'a rape episode' was one about a serial killer nicknamed Excalibur shown late last November. After her Peter had already assaulted four women.

Her Peter. His trial lasts all of 65 minutes. She spends it alone in his barrister's office, too upset to watch, too afraid to hear the full forensic horrors of his crimes. Hers and his elderly mother's are the only tears shed for him, apart from his own. He sobs just the once, pleading guilty to six charges of rape, one of buggery and two of unlawfully wounding. The best his defence counsel can do isn't much better than the bogus *Kojak* theory. A flimsy portrait of an innocent man corrupted by pornographic magazines and films. Honest, M'lud, he'd never have done it were it not for a few copies of *Fiesta* and a butcher's at *Bistro Bordello*.

'To use his own words, after watching these films, "It was like a living hell in another world. I think the films control you. I just had to do something."'

Mary Whitehouse might buy it but Justice Melford Stevenson doesn't.

'I do not think I would be doing my duty if I didn't impose a sentence of imprisonment for life,' he rules. 'I express the opinion that in the context of this case life ought to mean life. I realise this opinion will horrify large numbers of well-meaning people but I am satisfied it is right. *Put him away!*'

And away he is put. In a new maximum security unit in Wormwood Scrubs, specially built for convicts like him with a one-way ticket. Ten years ago there were less than four hundred lifers in the whole country;

now that they've stopped hanging them there's over a thousand. Peter had better quickly get used to it. He has seven concurrent life sentences. One for each of the women he raped.

Life for Frances, a secretary, aged 22. After his assault he asked her, 'Did you enjoy it?'

Life for Anne, a student, aged 20. She cried, 'You're hurting me.' He laughed, 'That's good.'

Life for Janet, a music student, aged 18. He told her, 'I'm going to murder you', bit her on the breast, then sodomised her on the college lawn.

Life for Elizabeth, a student teacher, aged 20. He blindfolded her, raped her, then told her, 'I've got VD.'

Life for Shelley, a telephonist, aged 21. He slashed her as she tried to resist. Her wounds required 33 stitches. She asked, 'Why are you doing this?' He answered, 'I don't know.'

Life for Gail, a student, aged 23. The first one he attacked wearing his new leather hood. He threatened to slit her throat, raped her, then trussed her up like a chicken.

Life for Amanda, a student, aged 21. He stabbed her in the stomach and told her, 'I hate you.' When it was over he said he hoped she got pregnant.

Seven life terms for seven women. Some small consolation for his victims that Peter Samuel Cook will definitely die in prison, even if the majority of people still wish the evil little bastard had hung. But then the majority of people don't know he does. As bad a joke as any you'll hear in the charts, but three miles from his new cell block, come look for yourself. There, dangling from a T-shirt rail in a shop on the King's Road.

See the Cambridge Rapist swing.

UNABLE TO FINISH HIS OWN SONGS, David kills time singing someone else's. One of Nina Simone's. He met her last year in an Upper East Side New York discotheque during a break in his *Diamond Dogs* tour. He told her she was a genius and in the same breath admitted he wasn't. Nobody heard her disagree.

Nina didn't write 'Wild Is The Wind'. The music is by Dimitri Tiomkin, who composed scores for Capra and Hitchcock, the words by his lyric partner Ned Washington who wrote 'When You Wish Upon A Star' for Disney. Together they won an Oscar for their theme to *High Noon* and another nomination for 'Wild Is The Wind', the haunting title overture to a cheerless Paramount drama about a widowed sheep farmer who marries his dead wife's sister. The film version, a Brontë-esque dream sung by Johnny Mathis, gusted by in under two-and-a-half minutes. Nina's later version raged for a full six and sounded like a funeral mass. That's the arrangement David wants to cover.

The band play it straight. There's no other way to play it, even with electric instruments and a drum kit. No showboating, no overstatement, just the notes as written by a Russian émigré. It shows. 'Wild Is The Wind' blows in from the Urals, a folk song of the steppes to be trembled on balalaikas in the frostbitten depths of a peasant winter. Music of a hills-old European melancholy, its chords sighing with the same doomed passion of a Chopin prelude or Shostakovich at his most fatalistic. You wouldn't mess with their melodies and there's no need to mess with this either. Knowing their place, the band lay low in the shadows. This is a singer's song.

It's also a romantic's song. That's what makes David's decision so strange. A love song sung by a man devoid of any except that for fluffy white crystals.

'Wild Is The Wind' eats its heart and spills its guts. *Love me or I'll die!* It holds a rose in one hand and a dagger in the other, and if the rose isn't taken, the dagger's plunging straight in its chest. It's a suicide note dressed up as a sonnet. Love is not a summer's day or a moonlight drive. Love is a force ten gale and it will totally destroy you the same way Hurricane Hermione destroyed David when he was 22. The one time he fell, good and proper, and the bitch damn near broke his neck. Press the right nerve and he'll still bring it up in interviews.

'I was in love once, maybe, and it was an awful experience. It rotted me, drained me, and it was a disease. Hateful thing, it was. Being in love is something that breeds brute anger and jealousy. Everything but love, it seems.'

But that's not David talking. That's the Merck and the Duke and the switched-on Bowieness whenever there's a tape recorder in the room. That's not who sings 'Wild Is The Wind'.

BOWIEODYSSEY75

David Jones sings 'Wild Is The Wind'. The real David in his real voice. The one he used all the time back when everybody said he sounded like Anthony Newley, because he did. No role play, no pretence, not his Ziggy voice or his rock'n'roll voice or his *Young Americans* voice, the one he now describes as 'plastic', but the voice of the son of an estranged mother, husband to a separating wife, distant father to an overseas child. A grown man of 28 who sacrificed love for success, sex and drugs, now caught in the moment of trying to remember why in A minor. It's still a performance but, unlike 'Golden Years', it is not an act.

'Love me, love me . . .'

Except he hasn't any to give in return. All he has is pallid flesh, icy blood and an empty cavity behind his sternum. He's a vampire serenading a tombstone. Nina took it to the cemetery gates but David takes it further, beyond the grave: the Abominable Dr Phibes pining for his deceased Victoria. That's not romance in his voice. It's defeat and despair, the bleak realisation that the wooing hour has passed. The love he sings of is already dead. Like his soul. Rotted, drained and diseased.

Physically, morally, emotionally, the man who completes it perfectly in the first take has never been such a poor example of his species. And still 'Wild Is The Wind' is the most human record David will ever make. Maybe *the* best record he'll ever make. An old song, sung timelessly. No glitter, no make-up, no concept, not his words, not his music, just his voice. But that voice, deathly yet deathless, is enough.

That voice is life itself.

SIXTEEN

BLACKPOOL IS ALL A-TREMBLE. You can hear it in the waves lapping in from the Irish Sea. The tide bubbles up over the sand with a breathy *ah*, then rolls back out with an inhaling *ee*. Back and forth, back and forth, *ah-ee, ah-ee*. Beating along the Golden Mile like a drum, *ah-ee, ah-ee*. Plucking the overhead tram lines in pizzicato, *ah-ee, ah-ee*. Chiming through the rails of the Big Dipper, *ah-ee, ah-ee*. Jingling the filaments of every bulb in the Illuminations, *ah-ee, ah-ee*. Cackling in the jaws of the Fun House laughing man, *ah-ee, ah-ee*. Tolling from the top of the Tower like church bells, *ah-ee, ah-ee*. The whole promenade swaying with its rhythm, to and fro, *ah-ee, ah-ee*.

It's picked up by the gulls circling above Victoria Street, their piercing cries, *ah-ee, ah-ee*. And on the pavements below, oxygenating the hundreds upon hundreds of suited and skirted bodies scuttling into the Winter Gardens, breathing in, breathing out, *ah-ee, ah-ee*. White faces wild with an excitement that doesn't befit their middle age or mundane dress. The same untamed hysteria you'll see fizzing in the eyes of tartan-scarved teens busting ribs to clamber close to the Bay City Rollers. The eyes of idolatry.

This lot won't scream or storm the stage, but their hearts will beat just as fast a *thump-thump, thump-thump*. Because today they get to sit under the same roof as all their Rollers rolled into one. Organisers expect as many as 4,000 to cram in, while outside closed–circuit TV

125

BOWIEODYSSEY75

screens will relay live pictures to an estimated overspill of at least another thousand. In the foyer they're even giving out free colour photos to take home and frame by the bed or keep under the pillow, so all blessed enough to bear witness can forever snore sweet bluest dreams of the one and only.

Zzz-zzz!

Ah-ee!

Mah-ee!

MAGGIE!

Central Office have been saying it all week.

'This conference is the coronation of Margaret Thatcher.'

And she knows it. When she finally walks out onto the podium in the Empress Ballroom it's to a parping royal fanfare and a standing ovation. All rise for her majesty.

MAGGIE! MAGGIE!

She wears an electric Maya blue dress with wing collars and a pearl necklace, her blonde hair combed so far back off her face it looks like a wig trying to swan dive off the back of her head. She smiles indulgingly, exposing the sort of small stubby but sharp teeth a postman would fear in a Jack Russell. As she's being introduced, one of her subjects scampers to the foot of the stage with a gift. A blue feather duster, matching her outfit. 'To sweep out the socialists.'

The crowd applaud in ecstasy.

MAGGIE! MAGGIE!

Maggie, amused, tickles it over her lectern like Ken Dodd. Her fans fall to pieces.

MAGGIE! MAGGIE!

Licking out of her hand and she's yet to say a word.

She displays not an atom of fatigue considering her head only hit the pillow in the Premier Suite of the Imperial Hotel at 4.30 this morning. All week she's been furiously writing and rewriting her first conference speech as party leader, helped and hindered by different advisers, ending in an emergency redraft late last night, fine-tuning it way into the wee small hours. Forty-six typed pages, the first headed with her own handwritten note to self.

Relax. Low speaking voice. Not too slow.

She's timed it to around 35 minutes. The actual reading takes her 41, stalled by continuous applause and ricocheting bellows of simpering laughter. Joseph Stalin never had such an obsequious crowd.

Her every sentence is a 'Rule Britannia' sending them into rosette-flapping raptures, her voice like afternoon tea in a Royal Grafton Viceroy bone china cup. She attacks socialism, Labour and Wilson's government record as 'unparalleled in the history of political hypocrisy'. She champions free choice and free enterprise in a free economy with the freedom to be unequal in private health and education. She praises Britain as a nation that ought to be proud for having invented 'the computer, refrigerator, electric motor, stethoscope, rayon, steam turbine, stainless steel, the tank, television, penicillin, radar, jet engine, hovercraft, float glass and carbon fibres. Oh, and the best half of Concorde.' She preaches the rule of law and the continued support of British armed forces in Northern Ireland. The longer she speaks, the dreamier her apostles gawp, the more she transforms into Henry V before their very eyes; by the finale, all would gladly lay down their *Archers*-listening lives to follow her into the fields of Agincourt.

'We are coming, I think, to yet another turning point in our long history. We can go on as we have been going and continue down. Or we can stop – and with a decisive act of will, we can say, "Enough!"'

The ballroom roof shatters and the heavens open. Crutches are chucked away, cataracts vanish, bunions disappear, hernias untangle and the taps in the toilets gush forth with silkiest Bordeaux. The standing ovation hollers and hosannahs and claps its palms raw for a solid five minutes.

MAGGIE! MAGGIE!

The coronation is complete. The verdict unanimous. In the words of one evening paper headline: 'MAGGIE WEARS CROWN'.

Her hour is now, but then it was always going to be. Earlier this week, an independent Marplan opinion poll found that if held tomorrow she would win the next general election. Comfortably.

Tomorrow there will be no such ballot, though less than a couple of hundred yards from Maggie's front door, in Chelsea Town Hall on the King's Road, there will be the AGM of the National Front. The police will be there, not to stop it but to protect it from a large crowd of demonstrators chanting 'FASCISTS OUT!' Seventeen of them –

BOWIEODYSSEY75

International Socialists, the Union of Liberal Students, the Squatters and Tenants Association and members of the West London Campaign Against Racism and Fascism – will end up truncheoned and cuffed in the back of a police van while dead-eyed men watch from the Town Hall windows and laugh and wave and stiffen their arms in defiant Nazi salutes. All this while the day's *Mail* huzzahs for 'MAGNIFICENT MARGARET!' and the *Sun* pledges *'to make Britain great again'*. An extreme right front, coming up and sweeping everything off its feet.

Just what David wished for.

THE CLOCK TICKS BUT IT MEASURES NOTHING. It's just a hand jerking round in circles on the studio wall. It could be day or night, but in the brown cave of Cherokee nobody can tell and nobody needs to know. Time is abstract. David is either here or not here and even when he's here he's usually not here but over *there*, where he'll stay speeding in the fast lane of infinite possibility until he decides he's had enough. Of music, of staying awake, of empty vials and bloody nostrils. That could take ten hours, fifteen, more than twenty. There's no point in counting. His work is done when it's done or at least until he can't do any more. Then he'll show up again three days later and do it all over again from the beginning.

Somewhere and somehow amidst these nameless nocturnes of absence and exhaustion more songs appear like shoots of grass from the shifting dunes of hydrochloride. So much it really deserves a shared composer credit.

'All songs by Bowie/Merck.'

New riffs are scavenged from the old and borrowed. A teenage memory stuttering *'oh! oh! oh! oh! oh!'* along to the Yardbirds' 'Good Morning Little Schoolgirl' is spliced with a chorus hewn from his own 'Sweet Thing' to make 'TVC 15'. He cuts it the week Springsteen is in town playing four nights at the Roxy when he's able to steal his piano player, Roy. Without him swinging between the staves like Basie, 'TVC 15' would sound like a twelve-bar blues played with audible reluctance by a band who'd rather funk. It's David's idea of light relief, a rock'n'roll nightmare about a guy whose television eats his girl. Something Iggy hallucinated for real, as only Iggy could, then later told him about, not that he'll get his due 'Pop' in the brackets. It crashes somewhere between Lou Reed and *The Twilight*

Zone; 'I'm Waiting For The Man' and the episode 'Little Girl Lost' about a child stuck in the fourth dimension. Groovy, but disturbed.

So is 'Stay', a piece of glued-together shrapnel from *Young Americans*, recycling his Philly makeover of 'John, I'm Only Dancing' which never made the album. It's 'Golden Years' without the pink ribbon around it. A dirty night on the tiles spent sweating with sleazy dealers and fucking in toilet cubicles. It sounds sexy, but when you get up real close you can smell the cheap cologne. Then see the tears of the disco Casanova crying himself to sleep in an otherwise empty bed. That's drugs for you. They throw you up so high they forget to catch you – and there's no such thing as a soft landing.

The only challenge to Merck's contribution is from the opium of the masses. Again, that's drugs for you. However soft you start, it always leads to the harder stuff. Today, a nickel bag. Tomorrow, the King James Version. 'Word On A Wing' is David's musical mezuzah, a melodic love song to God from a born-again sinner. It's no 'How Great Thou Art' but it's better than 'Kumbaya'. A lot better. Just a shame with a tune that pretty he wouldn't rather have sung about somebody else.

Five songs now finished, it still isn't enough for an album. Measuring nothing, the clock ticks on.

BACK IN THE LAND OF TINNED KIDNEY SOUP, November the fifth passes with a whimper as England pedals ever backwards to the good old days of 1605.

The night after the bonfires fizzle out, Bird's Eye-belching Brits flop in front of another cutting-edge edition of *Top of the Pops*. Among the radical bill of fare introduced by the 49-year-old Jimmy Savile: ex-Traffic man Jim Capaldi schmoozing a 1960 Everly Brothers tune; Coventry DJ Pete Waterman dressed as a First World War infantryman groaning the 1917 music hall favourite 'Good-bye-ee!'; Gary Glitter orangutanging the 1962 novelty rocker 'Papa Oom Mow Mow'; the Rubettes oo-wah-ooing another of their early Sixties doo-wop pastiches; Billy Connolly taking the piss out of a 1968 Tammy Wynette hit; Pan's People dancing to John Lennon's four-year-old 'Imagine'; and this week's 'brand new' number 1 – 'Space Oddity' by David Bowie.

BOWIEODYSSEY75

In a reverse-gear nation where the biggest-selling album is Jim Reeves' *40 Golden Greats* and *Gone With the Wind* is back in cinemas, David – that is, an old David trapped in the moonshot formaldehyde of 1969 – is finally top of the singles charts. Part of a comfort-blanket culture woven from the been-and-gone, sentimental distractions from a much too unpleasant present. Give them old songs, familiar songs, sad songs, love songs, songs from the space race that's long since stopped, songs by Laurel and Hardy about lonesome pines, just give them *something* to forget that yesterday is gone and tomorrow looms like a bottomless pit.

But though the fireworks have finished, tonight, not long after 'Space Oddity' fades and the *Pops* credits roll, there comes a bigger bang.

Tonight, a bomb explodes.

This one has nothing to do with the IRA. Nothing that was made in their attic-flat bomb factory on the corner of Crouch Hill and Shaftesbury Road. Nothing like the one they'll throw through the window of Scott's Oyster Bar next week, packed with ball bearings, killing one diner and injuring fifteen others. Nothing that deadly, if no less powerful.

A different sort of bomb. Not the kind that brings fire engines, police cars and ambulances. Anyone stood outside the building on Charing Cross Road where it detonates won't even know it's gone off. Nor next door in the Jacey cinema, where the only tremors are in the pockets of dirty raincoats ogling a double bill of *The Nun and the Devil* and *The Lustful Vicar*. But it blows all the same.

Shortly after eight o'clock on the top floor of Saint Martin's School of Art, blasting the eardrums and eyeballs of around 20 casualties, mostly students. A 4-kilowatt human bomb, variously dressed in splattered jeans, baggy pinstripes, T-shirts, denims, safety pins, braces and a pink leather top, loaded with a bass amp stolen from David Bowie and a Les Paul inherited from the New York Dolls. Listed on the poster as '+ support band' to tonight's 50p headliner, Bazooka Joe, a rock'n'roll revival group who by the time they get to pluck a note won't have anything worth reviving. The bomb makes certain of that.

Whatever they or anyone else think rock'n'roll is, this blows it to pieces. Reminds Bazooka Joe that rock'n'roll isn't a groomed pet on a leash but a savage animal, feral and ferocious. Opens the door of the cage and sets it free again. So free, it's frightening. Familiar tunes by

SIMONGODDARD

The Who and Small Faces running filthy and naked, swinging screaming through the jungle canopy pissing and shitting on everything below. Others delivered in snarling hyena laughs about being lazy sods and 'WE DON'T CAAARE!' The call of the wild so vicious, so deafening, that after 20 minutes its roar is silenced by the panicky switch of a plug socket.

Which might end the explosion, but its dust will never settle. Not now the dream has finally come true.

Someday, maybe a real *uprising will emerge – a group of heroic young rascals angry enough to crash the Zeppelin, say no to Yes, void the Floyd and put Wakeman to sleep.*

Remember, remember the sixth of November.

The someday of the Sex Pistols.

SEVENTEEN

IF THEY'D KNOWN WHAT THEY WERE LETTING THEMSELVES IN FOR, they'd have thought twice about inviting him on. They thought he'd be like Elton, the first limey white dude granted a guest spot on *Soul Train* six months ago. Elton turned up in his glittery Elton clothes, took questions from the audience in his mild Reg from Pinner way, belted out two of his swingingest Elton hits and everyone had the funkiest, bumping, low-riding time. The funny thing being that behind the twinkly specs and flash suits by Tommy Nutter, the inside of his head was like a freshly shaken snow globe. Elton just hid it very well.

David can't. He's wired as a timebomb and the kids who've been bussed in from South LA to the studio off Sunset for free fried chicken and the chance to dance their pants off on Saturday morning TV can tell.

So can Don Cornelius. *Soul Train* is his baby. He created it, he hosts it, he produces it and he sells the advertising. Don is from the Southside of Chicago, served eighteen months in the Korean War with the US Marines and speaks in a voice so low it could trigger an earthquake early warning system. He's also got six inches on David and while his catchphrase might be 'peace, love and soul' Don doesn't take crap from anyone. Seeing David is high as the light atop the Capitol Tower he takes his skinny white ass aside and lays down the law.

'Brother? You know there are kids lining up to do this show who have fought their *whole lives* to try and get a record and come on here.'

His words make no difference. David is much too far gone a cocaine cunt.

He's dressed more or less the same as he was on *Cher*, in a blue suit and yellow shirt straight off the shop-window mannequin. He takes questions from Don and the audience, answering each like a hophead in police interrogation only vaguely aware of his surroundings, laughing at nothing worth laughing at in demented bursts. He mimes to 'Golden Years', the new single expected to be in the charts when this airs in January, and his last one, 'Fame'. He bangs his gums together to match the words as best he can. When he can't remember them he just bangs them any old way. Most of the kids in the studio are too busy making sure the cameras catch their Slauson Shuffle to notice. But the viewer will.

In plain sight for all the world to see. *This* is what 1975 has done to David Bowie. The aggregate of twelve months of lawyers and Hollywood and Hitler and Kabbalah and witches and Satan and Jesus and drugs and drugs and drugs and drugs and drugs and drugs and drugs and drugs.

All of it now crushing down like so much compacted garbage into a solid singularity. The spooks in his brain, tormenting him like Newton's wall of TV sets.

'Get out of my mind, all of you!'

The bottles of piss he may or may not have kept in his fridge. The bubbling Devil he may or may not have exorcised from his pool. The sky-high truths that might be splat-flat lies, but even if they're lies, they'll always be the lies that tell the mad sick truth of what happened to David Bowie in 1975. Because it can't have been in vain. He needs *something* to justify all the agony, the waste, the sobbing days of paranoid lunacy and the overdosing nights quivering close to death. Even if just *one* piece of art.

One song.

He's always described himself as a singer who acts out his songs when he sings them. Only this year he fucked up. He went Stanislavski method. He lived it for real before he'd written a word.

With Ziggy, he wrote the song first then found the clothes to fit the character. With the Thin White Duke he's got it the wrong way round.

BOWIEODYSSEY75

He's become the Duke with no song to sing, acting out a part before he's scribbled any script. Wearing the Duke's suits, combing the Duke's hair, sucking in the Duke's Aryan cheeks, smoking the Duke's cigarettes with the Duke's bony fascist fingers. Turned himself into a cold, vain, selfish aristocratic shit. And for what?

One song is all he needs. The singularity. A musical Duchy where he can cast him out and leave him to rot for all eternity. A safe deposit box he can put a lid on and lock away tight, peeking in again only when he wants to remember all the things he'd prefer to forget about the person he was when he wrote it. A permanent record for future reference, like a scar he can run his fingers across, close his eyes and picture the unstitched freshness of the gaping wound. It can't be anything small or subtle. It needs to be something giant, sombre, almost Gothic, provoking the same dry-mouthed awe as a medieval altar painting. Dark skies, crowns of thorns, bloody stigmata and shawled women howling at the feet of the dead Christ. It's the only way the Duke will relax his death grip and leave him be. He needs to write him a masterpiece.

David doesn't cut any corners. The Duke demands an epic and that's what he gives him.

A ten-minute monster.

Not a song, more a suite. It's not all one tune and not all one tempo. It's not rock'n'roll, though it has feedbacking guitars, and it's not soul, though in places it has a funky rhythm section. It's not composed purely of notes but sounds. It might be the kind of music Kraftwerk would make if they suddenly decided they wanted to be Led Zeppelin, or vice versa. It steals ideas from both but sounds like neither.

You don't so much hear it as see it. It's a film pretending it's a rock song and almost gets away with it. It's not in colour but in black-and-white. It's a silent movie but loud as hell. The script is in English but the subtitles German. It's directed by David Bowie but it could be Fritz Lang or F. W. Murnau.

It's a two-reeler, the drama evenly split. Scene one is the proletariat, opening like a ghost train, picking up galley-slave pace, the rhythm lurching like the shuffling worker drones of *Metropolis*. Scene two is the bourgeoisie, zigzagging off into a totalitarian disco: get down, '*Sieg Heil!*' and let them eat cake. As the music fades to black, the Schutzstaffel are still dancing.

SIMON GODDARD

The words aren't about anything other than how it feels to be the Thin White Duke. Something only David knows, something only he's lived, words only he will ever fully understand. A song only he can sing in the voice of Scott Walker smashing glass in Mosley's jackboots. To anyone else, the lyrics are an impenetrable cypher, a jumble of random phrases underlined from a year's dangerous reading of voodoo hoodoo, signifying nothing. The only word of any worth is '*cocaine*'. There it is. Twice. For the record, on the record. That's what this song is. A 10-gram panic attack.

He could have called it 'The Return Of The Thin White Duke', like the memoir he's abandoned, and maybe should have. Fondling the cross around his neck, David settles instead on 'Station To Station' as in the fourteen stages of the crucifixion. The theme tune to his own.

As his nominated title track, it completes the new album. It only has six songs, but this is one of them and 'Wild Is The Wind' is another, and the four that lie between hold their own with immaculate poise. It near killed him to make it, but in not quite dying for his sins, David shifts the musical Tectonic plates at the end of a year when they looked locked solid. Now that he has, there's no shifting them back. All genies out of their bottles, the hard work of 1975, his and others, is done.

In London, the Sex Pistols.

In Düsseldorf, Kraftwerk.

In New York, *Horses*.

In LA, *Station To Station*.

The second half of the Seventies can finally begin.

THE FIRST HALF PERISHES IN A MASSIVE SEIZURE. The worst bits of the last five years of rock music attacking all together at once. The stink of heavy metal, the pretensions of prog, the theatricality of pseudo-glam and the wet balladry of 'Candle In The Wind' rupturing en masse in a six-minute cardiac arrest. A record that desperately wants to be 'Stairway To Heaven' with all the gravitas of 'Ernie (The Fastest Milkman In The West)'. Someone's idea of a joke that's no longer funny now that it's quadrilling at full speed to Christmas number 1. No band fears the coming of the Eighties more than Queen, and so 'Bohemian Rhapsody' stands as their perpetual state funeral for all that was shite 1970–75.

135

BOWIEODYSSEY75

But there's no escape from reality. If that's what Britain wants – a poor boy from a poor family, bleating to his mama that he's killed a man – that's what Britain gets.

'I shan't shed a tear. Life is full of shocks of all descriptions and they have to be faced. So I await my destiny. I hope from this writing someone somewhere, wherever it may be read, will pick up some good from my experiences. I am just one example of many bad ones. But who can say totally so?'

The handwritten bohemian rhapsody of Franklin Bollvolt from his Brixton prison cell.

Patrick David Mackay leaves it for the last time on the day 'Golden Years' is released. He is driven to the Old Bailey handcuffed in the rear of a guarded van, a dark grey suit, a dark blue shirt and a faint beard casting a dark shadow on his chin.

The trial doesn't take long. Patrick denies murder but pleads guilty to three counts of manslaughter by diminished responsibility – the cat woman he knifed to the floor in Chelsea, the old woman he strangled in Belgravia, the priest he brained to death in his bath in Kent. The plea is accepted.

A Home Office consultant psychiatrist tells the court Patrick 'had well-marked sadistic interests. This is exemplified in his attraction to Nazi insignia and a history of dictatorships.' A separate professor diagnoses him as being 'a psychopathic personality' though 'not insane'. In summation, the judge rules him to be 'a highly dangerous man' and sends him the only place he can. The new lifers wing in the Scrubs alongside the Cambridge Rapist. Last stop in the Year of the Monster.

All that's left is for the papers to do their public duty. Ramp up the horror, tsk–tsk in their editorials and spare no gory details in giving their readers something gruesome to chew over until *Jaws* opens on Boxing Day.

'THE MONSTER OF BELGRAVIA'.

The owner of a probation hostel in Finchley where Patrick once roomed tells the *Mirror*: 'He used to talk of Hitler as young girls talk of pop stars.' The Cowdreys collect their 15 minutes of fame in the *Sun* brandishing his prized wooden swastika. And the mother he once tried to strangle grieves for her lost child all over the Sundays.

'My son is not a monster,' she implores. 'He's just a very sick boy.'

Then straight from the lips of Freddie Mercury.

'Sometimes I wish he had never been born . . .'

EIGHTEEN

'ARE YOU THERE, DAVID BOWIE?'

The question is posed to a cumbersome television set resting on a table in the Thameside studios of London Weekend Television where it is eleven o'clock on a wintry Thursday morning. The same studio where David last sat not quite three years ago talking to Russell Harty.

Not quite three years later, Russell is still here and from the looks of it hasn't budged in the interim. The same haircut, the same dark blue suit, the same foggy understanding of time and place.

'Yes,' says the television.

David is there. On screen, via satellite, over 5,000 miles away in the studios of NBC in Burbank, the other side of the Hollywood hills where it's 3 a.m. – the bloodsucking middle of the night when David feels most alive.

With his Fanta-orange hair he looks popsicle delicious if polio skinny in a crisp white short-sleeved shirt, a conspicuous earpiece jutting out of his right ear and a silent Brazilian Mardi Gras drumming on his nasal mucosa. He smokes constantly, twiddling a pair of spectacles, which he never puts on, and a black pen which he occasionally drops to mark the sheet of paper on his lap. Around and behind him, the set of Johnny Carson's *Tonight Show* with its chequered easy chairs and painted backdrop of a nocturnal island landscape. The fugitive Thin White Duke on some

South American veranda, waiting for cocktails with his old Kamerad Josef Mengele.

When this finally airs, pruned and tidied, late tomorrow evening in ITV's London and Anglia regions only, it will be David's first UK television interview in the ten months since *Cracked Actor*. A major coup for Russell, not that he's done any more research on David since the pair last shook hands in January 1973. Which explains his first question about the earring David wore when they last shook hands in January 1973. David, a time-skipped transmission from November 1975, ignores it.

'How are you, Russell?' he asks his monitor. 'It's nice to see you.'

Talking to someone trapped inside a television feels a lot like his new song 'TVC 15'.

'It's very odd,' he'll later comment, very oddly.

Russell will agree, though seems to find it considerably odder, since the David he sees on his screen doesn't look anything like the David he saw almost three years ago in the flesh. Like his telly's on the blink.

'What colour is your hair?' asks Russell.

'Which bit?'

'The centre bit at the top, above where your nose would be?'

'Well, it's . . .' David tips his sunburst fringe towards the camera. 'What colour's it look?'

'*Wellll*,' teases Russell, 'it looks like something out of the end of *Straw Dogs*.'

The joke, if it was one, breaks on David's stony face like a sherry glass on concrete. He nods slowly, repeating Russell's words like a perplexed android. Does not compute.

'Something out of the end of *Straw Dogs*.'

'Right, right,' stutters Russell, eggy grin rigid as he nervously shepherds David towards The Scoop.

'You've got something up your sleeve for 1976?'

'Yes,' says David. 'I'm touring, but I'm coming back to England in May to play shows. And, uh, look at you. And look at England. And be there. Be English.'

'Again,' says Russell.

'Well, as always. But English in England.'

Russell quickly drops his eyes, consults the notes on his clipboard from 1973, then asks if he's going to be coming back as Ziggy Stardust.

'Uh huh,' drones David.

Russell – clearly impatient for the imposter on his TV to shave his eyebrows off, dab on some blusher and don a spiky red wig – persists.

'*Are* you coming back as that?'

'I don't know yet. I haven't even worked on it so I think it'll probably be a lot more spontaneous.'

'You haven't planned your wardrobe? You haven't planned a figure? You haven't planned an image, whatever that may mean?'

'I think the image I may adopt may well be me. I'm sort of, sort of inventing me at the moment.'

'You mean reinventing you, yourself?'

'Yes. Self-invented.'

'From the waist upwards?' purrs Russell.

'Yes,' says David. 'Jolly uncomfortable.'

The more Russell talks – his voice that of a plump middle-aged waitress in a Preston tearoom lazily reciting the contents of her sweet trolley – the clearer it becomes he doesn't have any actual questions. He has only quips and joshes, sniggering innuendos and silly wordplay, flirtatious tit for frothy tat. He asks David what clothes he's going to be wearing on tour. David says he's only thought about what songs he's going to sing. Any other interviewer might instinctively ask 'Which ones?' Flapping his fan like a giggling soubrette, Russell drops the ball and changes the subject.

'What's brought you back? Are you short of money or are you short of the feeding off live audience bit?'

'I'm short of England, more than anything else.'

'In what way? I mean, you do know that the England you left two years ago is not the England you're going to come back to?'

'Yeah,' ponders David, brow wrinkling. 'Well, this Thursday is nothing like last Thursday but it's just as important. I'd miss it if it wasn't after Wednesday.'

Precious minutes fritter by without a single revelation. Russell's every lazy byway of questioning – on 'the pop scene', on the Bay City Rollers, on stage dressing – lead to a series of cul-de-sacs of shrugs and frowns, stupid questions obliging stupid answers like a Victorian parlour game.

'Do you bore easily?'

'No.'

'What are you reading just now?'

'I can't remember. Oh, yes, something on heliothermal energy and an Enid Blyton.'

'Do you read them both at the same time?'

'Well, if my left eye was functioning, I'd read them both together. But as it is I have to devote my right eye to one book at a time.'

When David pauses to sip from a glass, Russell wants to know what's in it.

'Tree Top apple juice.'

'Is it good?' asks Russell saucily. 'Would you *spit* some across the satellite?'

David takes a swig. 'No.'

'Good. Um . . .'

And so it continues, two people having a conversation across two separate continents becoming two people having a conversation across two separate dimensions.

Legs crossed and cheeks blushing, Russell minces the title of *The Man Who Fell to Earth*, then makes an Abbott and Costello sketch of David's new single.

'The song is called "The Shape Of Things To Come".'

'No, it isn't.'

'No, of course it isn't . . . um . . . the song is called "Golden Tears".'

'"*Years*"!'

The two-handed farce is mercifully paused to play clips from both, including an exclusive preview of David's *Soul Train* appearance yet to be broadcast anywhere else.

'I was very nervous,' explains David. 'So I had a couple of drinks which I never do and really shouldn't have. It's lovely. It's very funny.'

Not half as much as this. In the year of *Porridge*, *Rising Damp* and *Fawlty Towers*, the funniest half-hour sitcom anyone will see on a British TV screen. Bar the one gag that does fall flat, butterfingered by Russell.

'You know, also, since you've been away,' he begins sheepishly, 'or quite recently, the newspapers have been having a bit of a bash at your mother . . .'

David stiffens.

'. . . and saying that she's a bit tearful from time to time, and that she's suffering a certain amount of anguish, and that she doesn't hear from you an awful lot. Is that eyewash, or is it real?'

David's eyes crackle with lightning.

'That's really my own business.'

Russell pokes the cage.

'And that's how it's gonna stay, is it?'

'Yes.'

The lightning fades. David forces a smile.

'I see you still have a keen sense of rumour, Russell . . .'

SHE SEES IT. Of course she sees it. She stayed up late, all the way through *Beryl's Lot*, the news headlines about the IRA murder of Ross McWhirter and *Police 5* to see it, curtains closed, volume up, puffing through as many cigarettes as he did. She noticed a scar on his chin which wasn't there before and she caught the lightning in his eyes when Russell asked about her. She knows that lightning. She calls it guilt.

There were many things Peggy didn't like about it, but not all of them David's fault. She was annoyed at Russell for asking her boy if he knew what a demob suit was. *Of course* David knows what a demob suit is! His father's used to hang in the wardrobe. Stupid man! But all the same, she was pleased Russell mentioned her, and doubly pleased she'd done what she had to do to make sure he did.

David only has himself to blame. She would never have *dreamed* of it if he'd thought to ring her, just *once*, but the seasons have flown, the lime trees outside have budded, flowered and shed their brackets, and in all that time the only place she's ever heard his voice is from her hi-fi speakers as she soaks through another packet of Handy Andies.

The breaking point finally broke back at the end of August. Standing in the newsagent, seeing David on the cover of that week's *NME*, his face occupying the whole page, wearing glasses and looking spookily like his father. The headline read: *'Watch out mate! Hitler's on his way back.'* Twelve pence the poorer, Peggy brought a copy home and read the interview inside, a buy-in from an Australian magazine where David

BOWIEODYSSEY75

talked about the moral collapse of society and how much he'd love a right-wing dictatorship.

Peggy was appalled enough to pick up her phone and dial the *NME*'s offices on Long Acre. She told them she thought her son 'a terrible hypocrite' and extended an invitation for one of their reporters to visit her in her little flat in Beckenham to set the record straight.

They did, sending Charles, the paper's chief Bowie correspondent, and Kate, a freelance photographer who snapped Peggy in one of her smartest floral smocks brandishing a framed photo of David, aged 12, in his school uniform. She told them she was thrilled they'd come by since she rarely has any visitors, let alone David who hasn't rung her in ten months and never even sent her a birthday card. She'd just turned 62.

'I must be the loneliest person on the street,' she whimpered. 'But I don't bear any malice. I *can't* bear him any malice because I love him too much.'

Then she sat down, sparked up an Embassy and told them everything they never wanted to know about one of their most bankable cover sellers but were afraid to ask.

'David said in a paper, I think it was the *Sunday Mirror* . . .'

It was.

'. . . that he left home at 15. That's a lie! He was at home until his father died five years ago. He's had a home *always*. His father supported him financially. He and his father were like *that*, but he didn't get on so well with me because I'm a very erratic person. My husband and I lived for David. We approved of his work. But when he was at Bromley Technical College he started getting rebellious. He seemed to resent it if I said anything to him, and it hurt me because I'm so sensitive. I used to burst into tears. If anybody mentions David, I cry.'

As for all this Hitler codswallop. 'He's changing his views about *everything* all the time,' she tutted. 'He's like a chameleon. There'll never be a dictatorship here and *why* he says he'd want one I don't know!'

These many maternal woes of Peggy Jones made the following week's *NME*: Keith Moon was on the cover, David's mum on page nine.

'A MOTHER'S ANGUISH – DAVID NEVER COMES TO SEE ME'

That anguish picked up by the *Evening Standard* . . .

'DAVID IGNORES ME SAYS HIS MOTHER'
. . . the *Sun* . . .
'MY "LOST" SON BY MRS BOWIE'
. . . and several others. This was the 'newspapers having a bit of a bash' Russell referred to. The 'business' David refused to be drawn on.

But Peggy isn't done. She enjoyed seeing her name and face in print more than she anticipated. A *somebody*, at last. Real fame, stretching far beyond the checkouts of Beckenham High Street, as she realised when her letterbox began flapping with envelopes from strangers across the country, disciples of David hedging their bets with the postie-confounding 'Mrs Margaret Jones, Beckenham, England', all passing on their love, their thanks, their poems, their O-level art drawings of her son as Ziggy Stardust. Her own fan mail. Because once the letters start coming, you never want them to stop.

Not everyone's interested in yet another aggrieved Bowie's mum scoop, but the *Sunday Express* are game enough to hear Peggy out. Especially now she has a new headline to offer.

'I SAW THE GUILT ON MY SON DAVID BOWIE'S FACE'
Because she did.

'When Harty asked David about me,' she tells them, 'David said that it was his business. But *I* saw a look of guilt on his face! I am his mother after all and a mother can see things like that.'

To the existing crimes of no phone calls and no birthday card she adds no Christmas card.

'I don't want *anything* from David,' she sighs, 'but it would be nice to *see* him again. He has changed a lot. He is giving a series of concerts at Wembley next May and I will go and see him there. If I can't get a free ticket, I will pay for one. I'll make sure that I get through to him there and talk to him again.'

The reporter nods sympathetically as she insists she's in no way *envious* of David. Oh, no! Not *her* living on her meagre state pension and *him* with all that money. Ha! Because it doesn't buy you everything.

'Especially health!'

If anything, she feels sorry for him, for his whole family in fact, especially poor Zowie, her grandson.

'And what about his wife?' they ask. 'Do you see much of her?'

BOWIEODYSSEY75

Peggy's eyes crackle with lightning.

'I last saw Angela in March. I went to the Ideal Home Exhibition with her. But then . . .'

She hesitates, pursing her lips.

The reporter coughs. 'But then?'

The lightning fades. Peggy forces a smile.

'But then we spoke on the phone,' she says curtly. 'And I am afraid we had words . . .'

FROM THE FLOOR BELOW HER, he can still hear Angie's voice bouncing down the stairs like a Slinky. These days David hears it less than he used to, if more than he'd like. It's rare to hear it in Stone Canyon at all since Angie hates the place. Mainly because she never chose it. Corinne did. Sound travels all too easily between its jerry-built walls and Angie's capitals come express delivery – Corinne's lowercase that bit slower.

They're both in the master bedroom, supposedly packing for David, who'll be spending Christmas in Jamaica. Downstairs, he's only vaguely aware of odd thuds and snapping voices, his brain throbbing uneasily as he mentally packs his own trunk with as much Merck as he can cram between his churning sea of troubles.

He'll be staying on in Jamaica for the New Year to start rehearsals for his upcoming tour. He doesn't particularly want to but he needs the money. He also needs to flee the States if he wants to avoid a $300,000 bill in unpaid taxes from Uncle Sam. Going back on the road is a short-term fix to both problems. Long term, he needs to find a new country of residence – as he's been advised, a new tax haven, the reason he can't return to England either. The only options are somewhere offshore in the Caribbean or Switzerland, where Angie went to boarding school and where she's just started house hunting for them.

He rubs a tired eye with the heel of his hand.

Angie. Poor faithful angel always coming to his rescue. So much for the fruits of International Women's Year. In the end, her play about the prostitute, *Razor*, never happened. Nor did the Ruth Ellis film. Nor her poetry book. Nor her hopes of playing the Marvel comic book heroine Black Widow in a TV series. She's just appeared on a Philadelphia daytime

SIMONGODDARD

chat show singing Gershwin, badly, and now says she wants to star in her own TV special. That won't happen either. She and David may live like separate planets, their elliptical orbits now aligning, at most, twelve weeks out of an entire year, but for all her breathless self-publicity she will always and only ever be 'Mrs Bowie'. As she was again last month, page five in the *News of the World*, saying she loves David more today than she ever has.

'I WOULD STILL FIGHT ANYBODY IF THEY EVER SAID ANYTHING BAD ABOUT HIM.'

Upstairs, a heavy object thunks. David flinches.

Yes. Angie loves him, but then he doesn't believe in that rotting draining disease, does he? To him, as he told *Rolling Stone*, she's simply 'a remarkably pleasant girl to keep coming back to'. Only when needs absolutely must.

He has Corinne now, the selfless facilitator of his selfish existence, her granite face an unfailing map of honour, truth and loyalty. Somebody he can trust even more to scoop up his shit with her bare hands, but with the added discretion never to whisper a syllable to the press, let alone pop up on the cover of *19* magazine, skirt raised, flashing a garter belt.

Another dull thud above. He pinches his nose, his temples pulsing.

Trust. There are so few people he can, anymore.

Corinne? Always.

Angie? Mostly.

His silly loose-lipped mother? Never.

His manager, Lippman . . . ?

David's no longer sure. He's tried, but the paranoid aftershock of Defries is like a recurring nightmare, each time the cold sweats shivering that bit colder. Relations with Lippman have strained after wasting the past month burning himself out back in Cherokee with his old friend Paul Buckmaster, the cellist who years ago arranged the strings on 'Space Oddity'. David played synthesizer, Paul played cello and both played their nostrils, left and right. The sleepless result was a score's worth of moody instrumental pieces he'd long understood would form the soundtrack to *The Man Who Fell to Earth*. Except now Lippman informs him Mr Roeg won't be using it. David expects Lippman to challenge Roeg for breach of contract. Turns out he can't. There never *was* any agreement between David and British Lion films to supply any score. David merely assumed

145

BOWIEODYSSEY75

it. Now he needs someone to face the firing squad other than his own sugar-frosted ego. Lippman will do nicely.

Upstairs, a crash, a shriek, each like an icepick stabbing his head.

David has heard enough.

He reaches the bedroom door just in time to see an empty suitcase boomerang through the air and rebound off a wardrobe. Had she not ducked, it would have rebounded off Angie. Unharmed, she straightens up, face like a shaken soda bottle. Cap aimed at Corinne, she lets it explode.

'WHO *THE FUCK* DO YOU THINK YOU ARE?'

Corinne, cheeks flushed, shoulders trembling, doesn't answer. Just switches her steely gaze to a soft plead and glances at David. The protector begging protection.

But he can barely see for the grainy white static blinding his eyes, nor hear for the white noise blasting his ears. Messerschmitt engines, Panzer battalions and a million marching Brownshirts. All senses blinding bright white like a flag of surrender. To a year of too many drugs. To a year of too many demons.

It's . . . too . . . late . . .

Turning from Corinne, David hurls himself at Angie.

'HOW DARE *YOU* TALK TO *HER* LIKE THAT!'

Angie blinks, confused. This isn't what she told the *News of the World*.

'HE'S NEVER YELLED AT ME AND I'VE NEVER YELLED AT HIM.'

But then this isn't David. It's the Duke.

And Angie would yell back were the Duke's hands not suddenly clamped around her neck. Big hands with slender fingers, digging into her throat, squeezing and squeezing until she can no longer breathe, the only sound in her ears her own choking and Corinne's cries of 'DAVID! NO!', her face turning blue, her lips turning black, her eyes swirling with the wrong kind of stars and the leer of the monster that once was her husband.

BOWIE**DISCOGRAPHY**75

February **'Young Americans'**
b/w 'Suffragette City'
RCA Victor RCA 2523. Reached number 18 in March.

March *Young Americans*
'Young Americans', 'Win', 'Fascination', 'Right' / 'Somebody Up There Likes Me', 'Across The Universe', 'Can You Hear Me', 'Fame'
RCA Victor RS 1006. Peaked at number 2 in the official UK album charts in April; in the separate NME album charts it spent one week at number 1.

May *Images*
Deram DPA 3017/8. First UK issue of gatefold double LP compilation originally released in America in 1973. Misleadingly packaged in a new sleeve featuring a contemporary photo of David live on stage in 1974, its 21 tracks were all recorded between 1966 and '67. An accompanying single (Decca F13579) coupled 'The London Boys' with the album version of 'Love You Till Tuesday'. Neither reissue charted.

BOWIEODYSSEY75

July   **'Fame'**
b/w 'Right'
RCA Victor RCA 2579. Reached number 17 in early September. In America, 'Fame' became David's first US number 1, spending two non-consecutive weeks at the top in late September and early October (interrupted for one week by John Denver's 'I'm Sorry').

September **'Space Oddity'**
b/w 'Changes', 'Velvet Goldmine'
RCA Victor 2593. Re-release of David's 1969 breakthrough hit as a budget three-track EP in a new picture sleeve as part of RCA's Maximillion series. Helped in no small part by the inclusion of the previously unreleased Ziggy Stardust *LP outtake 'Velvet Goldmine', it became David's first UK number 1 hit in November, staying at the top for two weeks – exactly six years to the month 'Space Oddity' first peaked at number 5.*

November **'Golden Years'**
b/w 'Can You Hear Me'
RCA Victor 2640. Charted in late November just as 'Space Oddity' was dropping out of the Top 10, eventually peaking at number 8 the week before Christmas (returning to the same position again in the second week of January 1976).

BOWIESOURCES75

The memoirs of Angie Bowie, *Free Spirit* (Mushroom Books, 1981) and *Backstage Passes: Life on the Wild Side with David Bowie* (with Patrick Carr, Putnam, 1993); Ava Cherry with Lisa Totem, *All That Glitters: The Ava Cherry Story* (Aquarius Press, 2022); Glenn Hughes with Joel McIver, *Glenn Hughes: The Autobiography – From Deep Purple to Black Country Communion* (Jawbone Press, 2011); Geoff MacCormack with foreword by David Bowie, *From Station to Station: Travels with Bowie 1973 – 1976* (Genesis, 2007) and *David Bowie: Rock 'N' Roll With Me* (ACC Editions, 2023); Earl Slick with Jeff Slate, *Guitar: Life and Music with David Bowie, John Lennon and Rock and Roll's Greatest Heroes* (Michael Joseph, 2024); Cherry Vanilla, *Lick Me: How I Became Cherry Vanilla* (Chicago Review Press, 2010); and Tony Zanetta, as detailed in his and Henry Edwards' *Stardust: The David Bowie Story* (McGraw-Hill, 1986).

Other works: Viv Albertine, *Clothes, Clothes, Clothes, Music, Music, Music, Boys, Boys, Boys* (Faber, 2014); Joe Ambrose, *Gimme Danger: The Story of Iggy Pop* (Omnibus Press, 2004); Nina Antonia, *The New York Dolls: Too Much Too Soon* (Omnibus Press, 2005); Paul G. Bahn, *The Cambridge Rapist: Unmasking the Beast of Bedsitland* (Vanguard, 2012); Timothy Green Beckley, *David Bowie, UFOs, Witchcraft, Cocaine and Paranoia: The Occult Saga of Walli Elmlark, the 'Rock'n'Roll' Witch of New York* (Inner Light/Global Communications, 2019); David Buckley,

Strange Fascination: Bowie: The Definitive Story (Virgin, 2000); Tim Clark and John Penycate, *Psychopath: The Case of Patrick Mackay* (Routledge & Kegan Paul, 1976); Tom Doyle, *Captain Fantastic: Elton John's Stellar Trip Through the '70s* (Polygon, 2017); Paul Duncan (ed.), *David Bowie in The Man Who Fell to Earth* (Taschen, 2017); Dion Fortune, *Psychic Self-Defense* (The Aquarian Press, 1973); Peter & Leni Gillman, *Alias David Bowie* (New English Library, 1987); Paul Gorman, *The Life & Times of Malcolm McLaren: The Biography* (Constable, 2020); Roger Griffin, *David Bowie: The Golden Years* (Omnibus Press, 2016); Jerry Hopkins, *Bowie* (MacMillan, 1985); Dylan Jones, *David Bowie: A Life* (Windmill Books, 2018); Lesley-Ann Jones, *Hero: David Bowie* (Hodder & Stoughton, 2016); Steve Jones with Ben Thompson, *Lonely Boy: Tales from a Sex Pistol* (William Heinemann, 2016); Brian King (ed.), *Lustmord: The Writings and Artifacts of Murderers* (Bloat, 1996); Wendy Leigh, *Bowie: The Biography* (Gallery Books, 2016); John Lydon with Andrew Perry, *Anger is an Energy: My Life Uncensored* (Simon & Schuster, 2014); Glen Matlock with Peter Silverton, *I Was a Teenage Sex Pistol* (Rocket 88, 2012); Cliff McLenehan, *Marc Bolan: 1947–1977 A Chronology* (Helter Skelter, 2002); Jordan Mooney and Cathi Unsworth, *Defying Gravity: Jordan's Story* (Omnibus Press, 2022); Charles Moore, *Margaret Thatcher – The Authorised Biography: Volume One, Not For Turning* (Allen Lane, 2013); David Nobbs, *The Death of Reginald Perrin* (Victor Gollancz, 1975); Chris O'Leary, *Rebel Rebel: All the Songs of David Bowie from '64 to '76* (Zero Books, 2015); Louis Pauwels and Jacques Bergher, *The Morning of the Magicians* (Mayflower Books, 1971); Mark Paytress, *Bolan: The Rise and Fall of a 20th Century Superstar* (Omnibus Press, 2006); Nicholas Pegg, *The Complete David Bowie* (expanded and updated edition) (Titan Books, 2016); Trevor Ravenscroft, *The Spear of Destiny* (Corgi, 1974); John Robb, *Punk Rock: An Oral History* (Ebury Press, 2006); Chris Salewicz, *Jimmy Page: The Definitive Biography* (HarperCollins, 2018); Christopher Sandford, *Bowie: Loving the Alien* (Little, Brown, 1996); Jon Savage, *England's Dreaming* (Faber, 1991) and *The England's Dreaming Tapes* (Faber, 2009); Tom Shone, *Blockbuster: How Hollywood Learned To Stop Worrying and Love the Summer* (Simon & Schuster, 2004); Patti Smith, *Just Kids* (Bloomsbury, 2010); Sylvain Sylvain with Dave Thompson, *There's No Bones in Ice Cream: Sylvain Sylvain's Story of the New York Dolls* (Omnibus

Press, 2018); Paul Trynka, *Iggy Pop: Open Up and Bleed* (Sphere, 2008) and *Starman: David Bowie: The Definitive Biography* (Sphere, 2012); Curt Weiss, *Stranded in the Jungle: Jerry Nolan's Wild Ride – A Tale of Drugs, Fashion, the New York Dolls and Punk Rock* (Backbeat, 2017).

Key period broadcasts and theatrical releases referenced: *Confessions of a Pop Performer* (Columbia Pictures, 1975), directed by Norman Cohen, screenplay by Christopher Wood; *Russell Harty* (London Weekend Television, 1975), episode broadcast Friday 28 November 1975, directed by Mike Mansfield; *The Man Who Fell to Earth* (British Lion Films, 1976), directed by Nicolas Roeg, screenplay by Paul Mayersberg, based on the novel by Walter Tevis.

Period newspapers and magazines. National: *Daily Mirror, Daily Express, Daily Mail, Daily Telegraph, Guardian, Ideal Home, News of the World, Nova, Observer, Radio Times, The Sun, Sunday Express, Sunday Mirror, Sunday People, Sunday Times* (and *Magazine*), *The Times, TV Times, Vogue*. Regional: *Blackpool Herald, Cambridge Evening News, Daily Record* (Scotland), *Evening News* (Edinburgh), *Evening News* (London), *Evening Standard* (London), *Evening Times* (Glasgow), *Press & Journal* (Aberdeen), *The Scotsman, Time Out* (London).

Pop/rock and teenage: *The Bay City Rollers Say Shang-A-Lang: A Fab 208 Special, Disc* (ceased publication/merged with *Record Mirror* at the end of August '75), *Fabulous 208* (as *Fabulous 208 with Hit and Melanie* until 16 August '75; as *Fab 208 with Hit and Melanie* from 23 August '75), *Hi! with Petticoat, Honey & Vanity Fair, Jackie, Melody Maker, Mirabelle* (with *Valentine*), *Music Week, New Musical Express, 19, Pink* (as *Pink & Music Star* from 25 January to 30 August '75), *Record Mirror* (as *Record and Popswop Mirror* until March '75; as *Record Mirror with Popswop* March to May '75; as *Record Mirror and Disc* from September '75), *Sounds*; with very special thanks to the archives of Tom Sheehan.

North American publications: *Albuquerque Tribune, Billboard, Cashbox, Creem, Los Angeles Times, New York Times, Playboy, Rock Scene, Rolling Stone, Variety, Village Voice, White Sands Missile Ranger*.

Enormous thanks to Maggie Abbott for her detailed account of David's casting process in *The Man Who Fell to Earth*, and to Laurence Myers for supplying his own recollections of the Century Plaza legal summit between

BOWIEODYSSEY75

David and Tony Defries. Aspects of Malcolm McLaren's involvement with the New York Dolls sourced from this author's previous interviews with Sylvain Sylvain, David Johansen and Arthur Kane in 2004.

For extra help and facilitating, thanks to Tom Doyle, Mariana Scaravilli, the Margaret Thatcher Foundation and, as ever, the staff at the British Library for all their efforts during the recovery period following their 2023 cyberattack.

BOWIEIMAGES75

FRONT COVER
Newton's law: David as *The Man Who Fell to Earth*, New Mexico, summer 1975 (© Studiocanal Films Ltd/Alamy).

IMAGES page 1
The capped crusader: David and his cross to bear, Los Angeles, 28 April 1975 (© Max B. Miller/Fotos International/Getty).

IMAGES pages 2–3
Top row (left to right): Telly Savalas as Lt Theo Kojak – by the autumn of '75 *Kojak* was the most watched TV show in Britain with an audience of 17 million (© Avalon/Getty); A showhouse dining room from the March '75 Ideal Home Exhibition, as visited by Angie and David's mum (© Shutterstock); The Newton haircut – Schwarzkopf colours chosen by David, styled by Martin Samuel – would define his image for the next two years over his next two album sleeves (© Studiocanal Films Ltd/Alamy).
Bottom row (left to right): A northern soul dancer cuts physical graffiti in Nottingham Palais, September '75 (© Mick Gold/Getty); Fantasy death sport – James Caan gets his skates on in *Rollerball* (© Silver Screen Collection/Getty); Reality death sport – a White Hart Lane casualty of Spurs 2 Chelsea 0, 19 April 1975 (© Mirrorpix).

BOWIEODYSSEY75

IMAGES pages 4–5
Beasts of England. Left: Brixton boy David Robert Jones (© Studiocanal Films Ltd/Alamy). **Right:** Grantham gal Margaret Hilda Thatcher (© Shutterstock).

IMAGES pages 6-7
Sex symbols of '75. Top row: Ubiquitous glamour model Gillian Duxbury – in '75 she posed clothed and topless for every Fleet Street tabloid, also appearing on darts flights, microphone adverts and in an episode of *The Sweeney* (© Shutterstock); A different kind of chest to bare, the Rolling Stoned soul of Patti Smith (© Charles Steiner/Getty); David crosses purposes filming a US TV advert for *Young Americans*, Los Angeles, 26 March 1975 (© Ellen Graham/Getty); Vitamin-deficient playground lust object, 18–year-old Bay City Roller Stuart 'Woody' Wood (© Jorgan Angel/Getty). **Bottom:** 'Clothes must have craft but truth loves to go naked' – SEX sells at number 430 King's Road (© London Picture Archive).

IMAGES page 8
Pretty vacant. David loses his mind between takes on *Cher*, CBS Television City, Los Angeles, 18 September 1975 (© Ian Dagnall Computing/Alamy).

ENDPAPERS
Exit strategy. David feels for a way out of the dilapidated Hotel Artesia, one of the principal locations for *The Man Who Fell to Earth* (© Studiocanal Films Ltd/Alamy).

Picture research and layout concept by Simon Goddard.

THANKYOU

Such is the support from where dreams are woven –
Marc Riley, Ted Kessler, Real Magic Books in Wendover
and everyone involved with the 2024
Bowie Convention in Liverpool.

The Omnibus kids from Fame –
David Barraclough, Millen Brown-Ewens, Greg Morton,
Neal Price and the great Debra Geddes at Great Northern PR.

Thin white Kevin Pocklington at The North Literary Agency
and electric lady Alison Rae for keeping the words on their wings.

And to Sylv – it's all in 'Wild Is The Wind'.

DAVID BOWIE
will return in

BOWIEODYSSEY76

COMING 2026